THE FINEST GARDENS OF THE SOUTH EAST

After studying forestry and horticulture in the early 1980s, Tony Russell's career with plants has taken him from Snowdonia to the New Forest in Hampshire, then to Westonbirt Arboretum in Gloucestershire – where he was Head Forester for thirteen years – and recently back to Snowdonia. Tony is a familiar face and voice on TV and radio, presenting a number of TV series such as *Garden Trail, Roots & Shoots, Britain's Great Trees, Saving Lullingstone Castle* and featuring on BBC Radio 4 in series such as *Invasive Plants* and on *Gardeners' Question Time*. He is also a regular contributor to the gardening pages of national newspapers such as *The Telegraph* and national magazines such as *BBC Gardeners' World Magazine*.

The Finest Gardens of the South East is Tony's seventeenth book and follows on from such bestselling titles as *The World Encyclopaedia of Trees, Westonbirt; A Celebration of the Seasons; Tree Spotting for Children, The Finest Gardens in Wales* and *The Finest Gardens in the South West*. He is also editor of the annual publication *Great Gardens to Visit* and the magazine *Discover Britain's Gardens*.

In addition to his broadcasting and writing, Tony runs a thriving consultancy that provides advice and guidance on gardens to private owners, charitable trusts and UK-wide organisations such as the National Trust. Tony is an avid botanical traveller and regularly leads tours for plant and garden enthusiasts to locations across the world, including the Himalayas, Amazonia, China, Japan, New Zealand and India.

For more information visit:
www.gardenstovisit.net
www.amberley-books.com

THE FINEST GARDENS OF THE SOUTH EAST

TONY RUSSELL

AMBERLEY

The Exotic Garden, Great Dixter.

First published 2016

Amberley Publishing
The Hill, Stroud,
Gloucestershire, GL5 4EP
www.amberley-books.com

Principal photographer Tony Russell; text and
photographic © Tony Russell 2016. Thanks to
Sue Liassides for both her photographic and research
work on this book.

The right of Tony Russell to be identified as the
Author of this work has been asserted in accordance
with the Copyrights, Designs and Patents Act 1988.

ISBN 978 1 4456 4978 8 (print)
ISBN 978 1 4456 4979 5 (ebook)

British Library Cataloguing in Publication Data.
A catalogue record for this book is available from the
British Library.

Printed in the UK.

Photo page 1 – Winkworth Arboretum

INTRODUCTION

Having spent the first twenty years of my life living in Surrey, some of the earliest garden visits I can remember were to gardens featured within this book. Along the A3 to the RHS at Wisley was one of my parents' favourite Sunday afternoon jaunts, as it was for my grandparents too. I have a clear memory of the old entrance gates long before the 'retail opportunities' started to appear. I also remember my grandfather, who was himself a great gardener, telling me about the social gatherings that used to take place at Polesden Lacey and how, when he was younger, members of the Royal family drove virtually past our house to get there – fascinating stuff for a lad still at school. Hampton Court Palace Gardens were an annual visit for my local Sunday school and 'us boys' always looked forward to the exciting prospect of deliberately losing ourselves in the maze for hours on end, much to the distraction of the Church ladies who had kindly offered to escort us on the trip!

Summer holidays were normally to the Sussex or Kent coastline and this too offered the chance of visiting gardens on the journey there and back. My initial discovery of Arundel Castle, Hever Castle, Petworth and Nymans happened in this way. Of course much water has passed under the bridge since then. The Great Storm of October 1987 probably produced the most significant changes to the gardens in South East England and with hindsight (although definitely not at the time) that event was helpful, allowing gardens to rejuvenate, be restored and replanted in a way that ensures their survival for at least the next century. Another change has been the 'opening up' of gardens that had previously been behind closed doors. There are significantly more gardens to visit today in Kent, Sussex and Surrey than there were forty years ago and this is undoubtedly to our benefit.

Kent has for generations been known as 'The Garden of England' and although this title is due more to its long history of fruit cultivation, it is a name that fits perfectly with our present inclination to go out and visit gardens, as it does for Sussex and Surrey too. It is no exaggeration to say that within these three counties there are more beautiful and horticulturally worthy gardens than in any other region of the British Isles. It is my hope that this book will go some way to encouraging even more of us to discover them.

Tony Russell
January 2016

❋ THE LIST OF GARDENS

❊ THE LIST OF GARDENS

FEATURED GARDENS

ARUNDEL CASTLE
Arundel, West Sussex
BN18 9AB
Tel: 01903 882173
www.arundelcastle.org

BATEMAN'S
Bateman's Ln, Burwash,
East Sussex TN19 7DS
Tel: 01435 882302
www.nationaltrust.org.uk/
batemans

**BEDGEBURY NATIONAL
PINETUM**
Park Ln, Goudhurst,
Kent, TN17 2SL
Tel: 01580 879842
www.forestry.gov.uk/bedgebury

BORDE HILL
Borde Hill Ln, Haywards Heath,
West Sussex RH16 1XP
Tel: 01444 450326
www.bordehill.co.uk

BROADVIEW
Hadlow College, Tonbridge Road,
Hadlow, Kent TN11 0AL, United
Kingdom
Tel: 01732 853211
www.broadviewgardens.co.uk

DENMANS
Denmans Lane, Fontwell,
Arundel BN18 0SU
Tel: 01243 542808
www.denmans-garden.co.uk

DODDINGTON PLACE
Doddington Nr Sittingbourne,
Kent ME9 0BB
Tel: 01795 886101
www.doddingtonplacegardens.co.uk

EMMETTS
Ide Hill, Sevenoaks,
Kent TN14 6BA
Tel: 01732 751509
www.nationaltrust.org.uk/
emmetts-garden

GREAT COMP
Comp Ln, St Mary's Platt,
Sevenoaks, Kent TN15 8QS
Tel: 01732 885094
www.greatcompgarden.co.uk

GREAT DIXTER
Northiam, Rye,
East Sussex, TN31 6PH
Tel: 01797 252878
www.greatdixter.co.uk

GROOMBRIDGE PLACE
Groombridge Hill, Groombridge,
Tunbridge Wells, Kent TN3 9QG
Tel: 01892 861444
www.groombridgeplace.com

HALL PLACE GARDENS
Bourne Rd, Dartford, Bexley,
Greater London DA5 1PQ
Tel: 01322 526574
www.bexleyheritagetrust.org.uk/
hallplace

HAM HOUSE & GARDENS
Ham St, Richmond-upon-Thames
Surrey TW10 7RS
Tel: 020 8940 1950
www.nationaltrust.org.uk/
ham-house-and-garden

**HAMPTON COURT PALACE
GARDENS**
East Molesey,
Surrey KT8 9AU
Tel: 0844 482 7777
www.hrp.org.uk/hampton-court-
palace

**HANNAH PESCHAR
SCULPTURE GARDEN**
Black & White Cottage, Standon Ln,
Ockley, Surrey RH5 5QR
Tel: 01306 627269
www.hannahpescharsculpture.com

HERSTMONCEUX CASTLE
Herstmonceux, East Sussex
BN27 1RN
Tel: 01323 834457
www.herstmonceux-castle.com

HEVER CASTLE
Hever Rd, Hever,
Edenbridge, Kent TN8 7NG
Tel: 01732 865224
www.hevercastle.co.uk/visit/
gardens

HIGH BEECHES
High Beeches Ln, Handcross,
Haywards Heath,
West Sussex RH17 6HQ
Tel: 01444 400589
www.highbeeches.com

HOLE PARK
Cranbrook Rd, Benenden,
Cranbrook, Kent TN17 4JA
Tel: 01580 241344
www.holepark.com

IGHTHAM MOTE
Mote Rd, Sevenoaks,
Kent TN15 0NT
Tel: 01732 810378
www.nationaltrust.org.uk/
ightham-mote

KING JOHN'S LODGE
Sheepstreet Ln, Etchingham,
East Sussex TN19 7AZ
Tel: 01580 819232
www.kingjohnsnursery.co.uk

**LULLINGSTONE CASTLE & THE
WORLD GARDEN**
Lullingstone Castle,
Dartford DA4 0JA
Tel:01322 862114
www.lullingstonecastle.co.uk

LOSELEY PARK
Guildford, Surrey GU3 1HS
Tel: 01483 405120
www.loseleypark.co.uk

MARLE PLACE
Marle Place, Marle Pl Rd,
Tonbridge, Kent TN12 7HS
Tel: 01892 722304
www.marleplace.co.uk

MOUNT EPHRAIM
Staple St, Hernhill,
Faversham ME13 9TX
Tel: 01227 751496
www.mountephraimgardens.co.uk

MERRIMENTS
Hawkhurst Road, Hurst Green,
East Sussex TN19 7RA
Tel: 01580 860666
www.merriments.co.uk

FEATURED GARDENS

NYMANS
Nymans Cottages, Staplefield Ln,
Handcross,
West Sussex RH17 6EB
Tel: 01444 405250
www.nationaltrust.org.uk/nyman

PAINSHILL PARK
Portsmouth Rd, Cobham,
Surrey KT11 1JE
Tel: 01932 868113
www.painshill.co.uk

PARHAM HOUSE
Parham Park, Pulborough,
West Sussex RH20 4HS
Tel: 01903 742021
www.parhaminsussex.co.uk

PASHLEY MANOR
Pashley Road, Ticehurst,
Wadhurst TN5 7HE
Tel: 01580 200888
www.pashleymanorgardens.com

PENSHURST PLACE
Penshurst Place,
Penshurst TN11 8DG
Tel: 01892 870307
www.penshurstplace.com

PETWORTH HOUSE
Church St, Petworth,
West Sussex, GU28 0AE
www.nationaltrust.org.uk/
petworth-house-and-park

POLESDEN LACEY
Great Bookham, Dorking,
Surrey RH5 6BB
www.nationaltrust.org.uk/
polesden-lacey

RAMSTER
Petworth Rd, Chiddingfold,
Godalming, Surrey GU8 4SN
Tel: 01428 654167
www.ramsterevents.com/surrey-
garden-tea-house

RHS WISLEY
Wisley Ln, Wisley,
Woking GU23 6QB
Tel: 0845 260 9000
www.rhs.org.uk/gardens/wisley

RIVERHILL HOUSE GARDENS
Sevenoaks, Kent TN15 0RR
Tel: 01732 459777
www.riverhillgardens.co.uk

SAVILL GARDEN WINDSOR
Wick Ln, Englefield Green,
Surrey, TW20 0UU
Tel: 01784 485400
www.theroyallandscape.co.uk/
gardens-and-landscape/
the-savill-garden

SCOTNEY CASTLE
Finchcocks, Royal Tunbridge Wells,
Lamberhurst, Kent TN3
Tel: 01892 893820
www.nationaltrust.org.uk/
scotney-castle

**SECRET GARDENS OF
SANDWICH**
The Salutation, Knightrider St,
Sandwich CT13 9EW
Tel: 01304 619919
www.the-salutation.com/
the-gardens

SHEFFIELD PARK
Uckfield, East Sussex, TN22 3QX
www.nationaltrust.org.uk/
sheffield-park-and-garden

SISSINGHURST CASTLE
Biddenden Rd, Cranbrook,
Kent TN17 2AB
Tel: 01580 710701
www.nationaltrust.org.uk/sissing-
hurst-castle-garden

STANDEN HOUSE & GARDEN
W Hoathly Rd, East Grinstead,
Sussex RH19 4NE
Tel: 01342 323029
www.nationaltrust.org.uk/
standen-house-and-garden

**ST MARY'S HOUSE AND
GARDEN**
The Street, Bramber,
West Sussex BN44 3WE
Tel: 01903 816205
www.stmarysbramber.co.uk

SUSSEX PRAIRIES GARDEN
Morlands Farm, Wheatsheaf Rd,
Woodmancote, West Sussex
BN5 9AT
Tel: 01273 495902
www.sussexprairies.co.uk

TITSEY PLACE
Titsey Hill, Oxted,
Surrey RH8 0SD
Tel: 01273 715378
www.titsey.org

VALLEY GARDENS WINDSOR
The Great Park
Windsor
Berkshire SL4 2HT
Tel: 01753 860222
www.theroyallandscape.co.uk/
gardens-and.../the-valley-gardens

WAKEHURST PLACE
Ardingly, Haywards Heath,
Sussex RH17 6TN
Tel: 01444 894066
www.kew.org/visit-wakehurst

**WEALD & DOWNLAND OPEN
AIR MUSEUM**
Town Ln, Chichester,
West Sussex PO18 0EU
Tel: 01243 811363
www.wealddown.co.uk

WEST DEAN GARDENS
West Dean, North Chichester,
West Sussex PO18 0QZ
Tel: 01243 811301
www.westdean.org.uk/gardens

WINKWORTH ARBORETUM
Hascombe Road
Godalming
Surrey
GU8 4AD
Tel: 01483 208477
www.nationaltrust.org.uk/
winkworth-arboretum

✳ ARUNDEL CASTLE GARDENS

In recent years there has been a trend for stately homes, castles and other historical properties to restore their gardens in an attempt to reach a wider audience and encourage more visitors. Where no such previous garden existed, property owners and managers have ploughed ahead undeterred with new garden designs and creations – with rather mixed results it has to be said. So, it is pleasing to visit Arundel Castle (a property which in 2006 did not even warrant a mention in the *Daily Telegraph*'s *Good Gardens Guide*) and be able to say that the new garden created here in the past few years has turned Arundel into one of best gardens to visit in the south-east of England.

At its heart is the Collector Earl's Garden, a flamboyant formal garden with both Jacobean and Italianate influences, designed by award-winning garden designers Isobel and Julian Bannerman as a tribute to Thomas Howard, 14th Earl of Arundel (1585–1646), who was one of the first great English art collectors and consequently became known as ▸

The Collector Earl's Garden.

◄ 'The Collector Earl'. This new garden occupies around one third of Arundel's original Georgian and Victorian walled kitchen garden, which by the 1970s was largely derelict and until the Bannerman's arrival used as a car park!

This new garden contains stunning green oak features, including columns, gateways, pavilions and a domed pergola, plus fountains, pools and cascades. The pergola and fountains are based on those seen in the background of a famous Mytens portrait of the Countess of Arundel painted around 1618, while the gateways and pavilions are influenced by Inigo Jones's designs for Arundel House dating from the early seventeenth century. Flamboyant this garden may be, but it is well researched and sits harmoniously within Arundel's historic setting.

The centrepiece is a rockwork mound, planted with palms, tree ferns, cordylines and large-leaved paulownias, upon which sits a green oak version of 'Oberon's Palace' containing shell-lined walls and a golden coronet 'dancing' upon a single water fountain.

The Collectors Earl's Garden is only part of Arundel's horticultural delights. The present Duke and Duchess of Norfolk have also transformed the rest of the walled garden, creating an organic kitchen garden, magnificent stumpery using old tree stumps from the estate, stunning herbaceous borders, a cut-flower garden, tropical glasshouse, wild flower garden and a restored Victorian vine house. Beyond the walled garden look out for the ancient cork oak tree *Quercus suber* and the rose garden near the castle entrance.

Garden designed by Isabel and Julian Bannerman.

The Cut Flower Garden.

✳ BATEMAN'S

*Our England is a garden that is full of stately
views,
Of borders, beds and shrubberies and lawns
and avenues,
With statues on the terraces and peacocks
strutting by:
But the glory of the garden lies in more than
meets the eye.*

'The Glory of the Garden', Rudyard Kipling, 1911.

Set in tranquil undulating and wooded Sussex countryside, Kipling first saw Bateman's in 1902. A solid Jacobean house dating from 1634, his impressions were positive: 'It is a good and peaceable place ... we entered and felt her spirit, her Feng Shui, to be good.' Soon after it became his home and remained so until his death in 1936.

Today it is one of The National Trust's most cherished properties and still captures the very essence of the man who, like his contemporary Thomas Hardy, has come to represent a crucial period within England's ▸

Batemans – 'a good and peaceable place'.

◀ past. Kipling was first and foremost an Empire man, who confidently embraced a world that was imperiously pink, only to find himself desperately trying to wipe the blood and mud of northern France off his hands. After his son Jack's death, Bateman's became his solace, his rock, his placement in a world that was quickly changing.

One of the main features of the garden, a pleached lime avenue, was planted in 1898, four years before Kipling's arrival. However the pond, the rose garden, planted in shades of pink and red 'Betty Prior' and 'Frensham', and the encircling yew hedges were all laid out to his design – a plan of which still hangs in his study today. The garden was paid for out of the £7,700 he received with his Nobel Prize for Literature in 1907.

How much physical work he did in his garden is up for discussion, but his ▶

The pond.

◀ designs clearly show his wish to link his Edwardian present with the past. Arts & Crafts attention to detail abound, with yew-green alcoves, beautifully crafted wooden seats, statuary, patterned brickwork paths and a sundial inscribed 'It's later than you think' sit comfortably alongside walled gardens of mulberry, quince and medlar, a pear pergola designed by Kipling on the eve of the First World War and a superb herb garden. Formal lawns gradually give way to a wild garden full of grasses, flowers and bulbs overplanted with trees and shrubs, which in turn run out on the banks of the River Dudwell where a riverside walk leads to a working flour mill dating from around 1750.

Pleached lime avenue.

❋ BEDGEBURY NATIONAL PINETUM AND FOREST GARDENS

The National Pinetum at Bedgebury, situated in the High Weald of Kent, currently holds one of the most complete collections of coniferous trees on one site anywhere in the world. In all there are over 12,000 listed specimens, made up of over 1,800 different species, including many rare, endangered and historically important specimens, growing across 320 acres (130 hectares).

Now to some, a collection of just 'pines' (which it is not) might at first sound rather uninteresting, but in fact the diversity and beauty to be found among the Bedgebury collection is really quite astonishing and is enhanced by the far-reaching views attained across the attractive rolling and sylvan topography of the High Weald landscape.

In truth, Bedgebury is far more than a collection of conifers. The Manor of Bedgebury dates back to a deed of Kenwulf, King of Merica in AD 815. Bedgebury Manor was home to Viscount Beresford and his family from 1836 to 1890. In 1840 ornamental grounds were established to the south of the Manor House (now in ▸

Marshall's Lake .

❁ BEDGEBURY NATIONAL PINETUM AND FOREST GARDENS

◀ private ownership), and these included lakes surrounded by ornamental plantings of rhododendrons and other exotic shrubs and trees, many of which were conifers. These still lay at the heart of the Pinetum today and there are delightful walks around Marshall's Lake, which is fringed by American swamp cypress *Taxodium distychum* and has a resident population of waterfowl.

In 1920, concern over the poor condition of conifers growing in the Royal Botanic Gardens at Kew led to a search to find a suitable location to establish a new collection away from London. By 1924 Kew and the Forestry Commission were jointly establishing a National Conifer Collection at Bedgebury, the estate having previously been purchased by the Crown in 1919.

Today, not only is Bedgebury a place of great beauty, it is also at the forefront of plant conservation. The Pinetum is home to over ninety vulnerable or critically endangered species and holds five Plant Heritage (NCCPG) National Collections: Yew, Juniper, Thuja, Lawson Cypress and Leyland Cypress. It also contains some of the oldest and largest examples of conifers in Britain. Much of the work carried out by Bedgebury and its staff is actively helping to ensure that endangered species are given as much protection as possible in the wild and that propagation material is collected and programmes put in place to build up the genetic stock, not just at Bedgebury but within other plant collections around the world.

Rhododendrons in spring.

Giant Redwoods in the Pinetum.

❄ BORDE HILL

Borde Hill is without doubt one of the most charming properties within south-east England. At its heart is a sixteenth-century light-stoned, red-tiled house, surrounded by 17 acres (6.8 hectares) of beautiful gardens, which will make the eyes of anyone with even half an interest in unusual plants sparkle. The gardens are in turn surrounded by 200 acres (80.9 hectares) of parkland and bluebell woods all set within an Area of Outstanding Natural Beauty.

In essence Edwardian in design, Borde Hill's gardens were originally created from 1893 by Col Stephenson Robert Clarke. Col Clarke propagated and planted seeds collected from Asia, Tasmania, South America and Europe by the great plant collectors of the early 1900s. Since then, four generations of the Stephenson Clarke family have passionately continued to develop what is now a Grade II Listed English Heritage Garden, renowned for its fine collections of rare shrubs and champion trees, including comprehensive collections of azaleas, rhododendrons, magnolias and camellias.

Borde Hill is partly laid out as a series of distinctive garden areas or 'rooms', which include an Azalea Ring and a fragrant Rose Garden which surrounds a circular pool and fountain fringed by Nepeta. Perhaps one of the finest features is the Italian Garden, which was originally the family tennis court! It was converted by Robert Stephenson Clarke in 1982 and has at its centre a formal rectangular pool, alongside which are terracotta pots planted with a succession ▶

The Italian Garden.

The Rose Garden.

◀ of colourful features including tulips in spring and geraniums and agapanthus in summer. The Italian theme is heightened by the use of golden box bordered beds full of pink pelargoniums in summer.

The Lower Terrace was restored in 1999 with the help of Heritage Lottery Funding and replanted to a design produced by award-winning garden designer Robin Williams, and from here there are fine vistas across the South Park and lakes. Several unusual trees and shrubs can be found around the Lower Terrace including the South American spiny shrub *Discaria chacaye* (formerly *Discaria discolor*).

The Upper Terrace has geometric-shaped beds edged with Myrtle *Myrtus communis* and planted with the evergreen fragrant, white-flowering *Magnolia grandiflora* 'Kay Parris'.

Other features at Borde Hill include a Camellia Walk, White Garden, restored glasshouses and a collection of rare southern-hemisphere plants where the old potting sheds used to stand. In the Long Dell Sino-Himalayan species surround Chusan palms and the Round Dell is a lush hidden area with further palms, bamboos and huge-leaved gunneras.

Spring at Borde Hill.

❁ BROADVIEW GARDENS

Set in the peaceful and picturesque Kent countryside, Broadview's 10 acres (4 hectares) includes a series of beautifully manicured gardens, each with their own special theme ranging from a traditional Italian garden and an Oriental garden, through to a sensory garden and a water garden. National Collections NCCPG (Plant Heritage) of hellebores (at their best in February and March) and flowering Japanese anemones (August until October) are also major features here.

Originally designed and maintained as a teaching resource for horticultural students at Hadlow College, Broadview Gardens are now open to the public for much of the year and are maintained by a dedicated team of gardeners supplemented by work-experience students and volunteers.

The garden is formed around a 328-ft-long (100 metre) double mixed herbaceous border backed by clipped yew hedges and fastigiate oaks. Off this border run two grass avenues lined with clipped hedges alongside which are a series of contemporary and traditional gardens designed and built by the students. It is these gardens which provide both diversity and ever-changing vibrancy to the landscape. There is currently a grass garden, a subtropical garden full of large-leaved bananas (*Musa* sp.) cannas and coppiced *Paulownia tomentosa,* a dry gravel garden and fountain garden. Elsewhere in ▸

Herbaceous borders backed by clipped yew hedges.

◀ the garden, a more naturalistic style plays out with a 1-acre (0.4 hectare) lake edged with marginal moisture-loving bog plants, leading on to wild flowers, meadows and woods.

Throughout the garden Broadview has been intelligently planted for all-year-round interest. Winter colour and interest is provided by attractive peeling-barked birches, drifts of coloured-stemmed dogwoods and winter-flowering bulbs such as early *Galanthus* sp. These in turn give way to spring displays of tulips, crocus, hyacinth and *Narcissi*, used both in formal bedding schemes alongside pansies and wallflowers, as well as drifting through the main borders and in the plant trial beds.

Summer is when the herbaceous borders come into their own with splashes of strident primary shades contrasting so well against the cool, green shade of surrounding trees. As part of Broadview's long-term sustainability, staff and students are continually experimenting with drought tolerant plants that also look good during dry summers.

As always, autumn is about foliage, with fiery shades heralding the final curtain call to the growing season, while late-flowering perennials such as asters and chrysanthemums do their best to pull flowering on into November.

A further bonus to this garden is the way that the majority of the plants on display are labelled.

Dogwood stems in winter.

Drifts of Alliums.

✤ DENMANS

Nestling beneath the South Downs escarpment, just 5 miles (8kms) from the Sussex coastline, lies Denmans, an influential garden created from the 1940s onwards by plantswoman Joyce Robinson to a design which she herself described as being 'a glorious disarray of flowers, shrubs and trees amid the peace of sweeping lawns'. Influential garden designer and author John Brooks MBE moved to the property in 1980 and over the past thirty-five years has both worked with and adapted Mrs Robinson's original 4-acre (1.6-hectare) garden in a way that has both moved the design on but at the same time stayed faithful to the original concept. 'I came here because I liked the feel of the place', said John in 2010, 'it had interest and intimacy and I liked the person from whom I took over'. Interestingly enough, John went on to say if he hadn't liked Mrs Robinson quite so much, would he have changed the design more? That we will never know, but what we can say is that the garden today is the culmination ▸

Intimate planting design.

◀ of seventy years work by these two people and that 'glorious disarray' tamed by sweeping lawns, is still very much part of Denmans charm.

The concept of the garden is simple: plant closely and with joyful abandon so that little soil can be seen and intermix natives and exotics, different forms and textures, flowers and foliage. The whole feeling is one of intimacy; here are ideas to steal that will be at home in your own garden, no matter how big or small your patch is.

Bold sweeping curves are important throughout, be it the lines between sward and burgeoning borders in the walled garden, or the sinuous meanderings of a dry gravel stream bed which runs through open grassland, before flowing into a natural pool overlooked by a delightful statue of a tousled-haired boy sitting upon the bank. The South Garden is a delight in spring with bulbs and wild flowers and in summer takes on a tapestry effect created by varying grass-mowing regimes. Sunny ▶

The South Garden.

◀ herbaceous borders are aplenty; some hot-coloured and bleeding reds and fiery oranges into the shadows of tree-canopied corners where grey-leaved hostas, purple ligularias and white campanulas slow the pulse and relax the mind. The Top Lawn is dominated by a beautiful specimen of *Acer palmatum* 'Sango-kaku' and the Victorian conservatory, which was completely rebuilt fifteen years ago, combines tender abutilons, aeoniums and other succulents with an aviary.

The boy by the pool.

❈ DODDINGTON PLACE GARDENS

Surrounded by wooded countryside in an Area of Outstanding Natural Beauty (AONB) on the North Downs of Kent, Doddington Place is a 10-acre (4-hectare) landscaped garden set in the grounds of an imposing Grade II Listed red-brick Victorian mansion built in 1870.

Perhaps one of the finest parts of the garden is the woodland garden, which in fact only dates from the 1960s when a tract of deep acid loam, fed by underground springs, was discovered. Given the location, high up on the chalky North Downs, this offered a surprising and indeed valuable addition to the garden allowing ericaceous plants such as rhododendrons and azaleas to be grown in open ground for the first time. Peak flowering for these plants is May and June, however other acid-lovers have been added to extend the flowering season, including camellias seen at their best in March and April and *Eucryphia* sp., which flower into late summer. Other plants include magnolias, spring-flowering bulbs, the American calico bush *Kalmia latifolia* and a pocket-handkerchief tree, *Davidia involucrata*.

In recent years, the original and substantial Edwardian rock garden with pools, constructed out of Kentish rag stone from a quarry near Maidstone in the years leading up to the First World War, has been completely restored. Many of the original plants, considered dwarf at the time of planting, had outgrown their positions and loss of overhead shade during the Great Storm of 1987 had only served to increase their vigour. So in 2005/2006 a programme of clearance was instigated, which allowed the original rock features ▶

Central pool in the Sunken Garden.

◀ to be revealed. Since then more rock has been incorporated, pools restored, viewing platform installed and young rock plants, alpines, grasses, dwarf shrubs and conifers planted.

During the winter of 2010/2011 the original formal sunken garden was redesigned to incorporate eight new beds and borders planted with a mixture of bulbs (especially tulips and alliums), roses, herbaceous perennials and in the beds around the central pond, drifts of white-flowering cosmos.

Other delights within this charming garden include a new dahlia garden, a recently completed brick and flint-built folly described by Sir Roy Strong as 'a piece of Hampton Court' and extensive lawns and avenues, framed by impressive clipped yew hedges, which through a combination of years of neglect during the Second World War and strategic pruning into amorphous cloud formations after the war, are now reminiscent of the 'wibbly-wobbly' hedges at Montacute House in Somerset.

Doddington Place and gardens.

✿ DODDINGTON PLACE GARDENS

Herbaceous borders in summer.

✤ EMMETTS GARDEN

Emmetts Garden was originally laid out by passionate gardener and financier Frederic Lubbock from 1890 until his death in 1927. Influenced by his friend William Robinson (author of the much acclaimed book *The Wild Garden*), who advocated the planting of exotic species within a natural landscape, Lubbock zealously collected flowering shrubs, as well as broadleaved trees and conifers, many recently introduced into Britain and purchased from the prominent nursery of the day – James Veitch & Sons. These he underplanted with naturalised bulbs to echo the beauty found in the bluebell woods which surrounded the garden. By 1917 Emmetts contained over 500 different types of trees and shrubs as well as an attractive Italianate rose garden and employed twelve full-time gardeners.

On Lubbock's death, the estate was purchased by Charles Boise, an American geologist who continued to develop the garden and who built a Westmorland limestone rock garden, which is still present today. On his death in 1964 Emmetts was given to the National Trust. Perhaps the biggest task undertaken to date by the Trust has been the clearance operation following the Great Storm of October 1987, which blew down many of Lubbock's original exotic trees and destroyed numerous shrubs growing beneath them. Since then the Trust's active programme of replanting is ▶

Bluebell woods surround the garden.

◀ gradually restoring the original character of the garden.

One of the finest times to visit Emmetts is when the roses are in flower in the recently restored Formal Garden. Varieties include hybrid musk 'Cornelia' and 'Penelope' and floribunda 'Escapade', 'Iceberg' and 'Cardinal Hume', all in association with plantings of *Nepeta x faassenii*. Rosa 'Cecile Brunner' is trained along rope swags on the terrace above, where *Eucryphia x intermedia* 'Rostrevor' and *Eucryphia glutinosa* 'Camelliiflora' also flower in the summer months.

Boise's Rock Garden was restored in the 1980s and at the time the lily pool was deepened to provide a head of water for a nearby fountain and cascade.

The warmth generated by sunlight radiation off the limestone means that the garden sustains a superb collection of half-hardy rock plants including many tender Mediterranean *Cistus*. Other plants in this area include New Zealand *Epilobium glabellum* and North American *Peltiphyllum peltatum*. The less formal North and South Gardens are where replacements for the storm-destroyed Lubbock flowering shrubs have been planted, including a vast collection of noteworthy rhododendrons, seen at their best in spring. To see Emmetts' remarkable tree collection at its finest, mid to late October is undoubtedly the best time to visit.

Bulbs on grassland outside the formal garden.

In the Rock Garden.

✤ GREAT COMP GARDEN

Great Comp, situated near Sevenoaks in Kent, is a beautiful 7-acre (2.8-hectare) garden surrounding an early seventeenth-century manor house. Despite the age of the property, the garden on view today was only created after 1957 by Roderick and Joy Cameron out of a neglected earlier garden plus rough woodland and paddock. They first opened the garden to the public in the 1960s and then in 1982 set up a charitable trust to safeguard the future of the garden and to ensure it remained open to the public.

The house is central to the garden, which has been cleverly designed to offer vistas across sweeping lawns and between island beds and borders back to its mellow-toned brickwork, while at the same time winding woodland paths entice visitors to explore further into the garden and around every curve and corner. Long grass walks, which intersect the beds and borders, offer ever-changing views to strategic focal points that include moss-clad statuary, a temple, tower and romantic ruins built from old ironstone dug up on site over the years. ▶

The Italian Garden.

Mellow brickwork provides the background to the garden.

◀ The combination of man-made infrastructure and luxuriant plantings works to great effect, enhancing the views of the garden while creating the perfect microclimate for an extensive range of exotic plants, many collected by the Curator William Dyson over the past fifteen years. It is he with two other full-time gardeners who look after the garden today – along with a small band of dedicated volunteers.

In spring the garden erupts into flower with scores of magnolias, rhododendrons and azaleas underplanted with drifts of hellebores, especially *Helleborus orientalis* and other spring-flowering bulbs. By summer it is Great Comp's extensive collection of salvias which dominate, bringing warmth and flamboyant fiery colours to the borders, along with the orange, reds and ochres of dahlias, kniphofias, crocosmias and fuchsias, all punctuated by ornamental grasses.

One of Great Comp's finest features is the Italian Garden, which houses a fine collection of Mediterranean and other semi-tender plants. Specimen trees in the garden include a dawn redwood *Metasequoia glyptostroboides,* a coastal redwood cultivar *Sequoia sempervirens* 'Cantab' and a yew in front of the house which was planted in 1840.

A nursery on site specialises in unusual salvias, including *Salvia* 'Love and Wishes' launched at Chelsea in 2015, as well as an excellent range of interesting hardy and half-hardy plants. In August each year Great Comp organises a summer plant show, with many other specialist nurseries in attendance.

The Mediterranean Garden.

❁ GREAT DIXTER

Great Dixter was the family home of Christopher Lloyd, influential gardener and garden writer who devoted his lifetime to creating one of the most experimental, exciting and constantly changing gardens of recent times. Since his death in 2006, Head Gardener Fergus Garret and his team have continued in the same vein, pushing horticultural boundaries but always with half an ear out for the learned whisperings of Christopher, who to this day never seems to be far away.

The garden surrounds a medieval timber-framed house, which is the centrepiece to the garden and seen from every quarter. It looks somewhat different to when Christopher Lloyd's parents purchased the property in 1910. Soon after purchase, Lloyd's father Nathaniel commissioned Edwin Lutyens to clear the fifteenth-century house of later alterations, revealing in the process the original splendour of the Great Hall. Further enlargements were undertaken and it was also Lutyens who laid out the bones of the present garden, to ▸

The Exotic Garden.

◀ which Christopher Lloyd noted that Lutyens' infrastructure 'always seems fluid, never stodgy'.

The first sight of the garden is the Front Meadow, bisected by a flagged path to the front door, itself framed by an array of colourfully planted containers and evergreen topiary. On either side of the path, deliberately cultivated rough grassland plays host to a succession of flowers and bulbs including wild daffodils, snakeshead fritillaries, early purple and spotted orchids and North American *Camassia quamash*.

From here there is a natural movement around the outside of the house and through a succession of gardens: the Barn Garden with original Lutyens fig growing ▶

A generosity of planting.

◀ against the barn wall, the Sunk Garden with its central water feature and the Blue Garden where Oxbridge-coloured lace-cap hydrangeas abound. Arguably the two greatest features at Great Dixter are The Long Border, where Lloyd's use of annuals, perennials, shrubs and climbers is a masterclass in plant combinations, and the Exotic Garden, which in its sheltered position cleverly uses flamboyant large-leaved foliage plants and tropical colours to recreate a mix of plantings from south of the Tropic of Cancer.

Wherever you are at Great Dixter two facts will jump out. Firstly, the generosity of planting means there are so many plants per square metre you feel as if you are wading through a flowing river of foliage, flower and textures, and secondly, the sublime use of colour. Nothing is perfect in this world but the colour combinations at Great Dixter get as close as is humanly possible.

The Long Border.

❋ GROOMBRIDGE PLACE

These award-winning gardens, half-hidden in a broad wooded valley just south of the Georgian spa town of Tunbridge Wells, overlook a handsome moated red-bricked and tiled manor house built in 1662 for Philip Packer, Clerk of the Privy Seal to Charles II. Remains of walls from an earlier 1230 moated castle provide a superb backdrop to seventeenth-century formal gardens, said to have been laid out by Philip Packer with the help of his friend, the famous diarist and horticulturist John Evelyn. In recent years, areas within the walled garden have been thoughtfully restored and an interesting mix of new plants added.

The highest terrace is bounded by a decorative brick and terracotta balustrade and offers striking views down across the walled garden to the manor house beyond. Against the south-facing terrace walls, segmented by a series of stone buttresses, colourful borders, full to overflowing with summer-flowering herbaceous plants, are backed by climbing roses and clever woody plant combinations including a purple smoke bush *Cotinus sp.* growing through a golden-leaved catalpa *Catalpa bignonioides* 'Aurea'. A grass path fringed by geraniums leads upwards to two garden rooms – the Oriental Garden and the Drunken Garden. The Oriental Garden was inspired by the colours of an oriental rug, while the ▶

Seventeenth-century formal gardens.

◀ Drunken Garden is full of misshapen topiary junipers and featured in Sir Arthur Conan Doyle's Sherlock Holmes novel *Valley of Fear,* where Groombridge Place is renamed 'Birlstone Manor'. A recreation of Conan Doyle's study is located at the entrance to the garden and gives a fascinating insight into the life of the author.

South from the terrace, a gravelled path leads between a striking avenue of twenty-four drum-shaped yews and towards the moated manor house and accompanying knot garden. Off to the left is perhaps Groombridge's finest feature, a White Garden created in the former kitchen garden. The centrepiece is a statue of Flora, the Roman goddess of flowering plants, and she gazes down upon billowing clouds of white roses, interplanted with white foxgloves and campanulas. Other features include a lake and golden privet maze, where a male peacock carries out patrols and guard duty. Below the garden a canal offers visitors the chance of a short narrowboat trip which leads to the Enchanted Forest – a woodland area with pools which has been overlaid with living art, land-based sculpture and aerial walkways designed by Ivan Hicks and Myles Challis with the aim of exciting and engaging children with the environment.

The White Garden.

Stone buttresses shelter plants.

HALL PLACE GARDENS

Located alongside the River Cray within Kent, but also within the London Borough of Bexley, Hall Place is a fine Grade I Listed Tudor mansion built almost 500 years ago during the reign of Henry VIII for Sir John Champneys, the then Lord Mayor of London. The mansion was constructed using stone from Lesnes Abbey, a nearby former monastery, and built upon the site of an earlier manor house which existed in 1241.

Since Sir John Champney's time, Hall Place has been the home for a number of well-known historical figures including Sir Francis Dashwood (a member of the notorious Hellfire Club), Edwardian music hall singer and actress Denise Orme and the socialite and friend of royalty the Countess of Limerick. In 1935 the municipal Borough of Bexley took ownership of the property, and today it is managed and maintained by the Bexley Heritage Trust, who in recent years, with the help of a £2million grant from the Heritage Lottery Fund, have restored parts of the mansion and garden and extended visitor facilities.

Inside the hall is a magnificent panelled Tudor Great Hall and Minstrels Gallery, and outside there are 35 acres (14 hectares) of landscaped grounds and award-winning gardens, which have won the Civic Trust's Green Flag award every year since 1996. In summer it is the long herbaceous ▶

The Tudor mansion.

◀ borders planted in cottage-garden style which command attention, along with rose gardens, an Italianate sunken garden, a grass maze and a rock and heather garden made from 95 tonnes of Kentish Rag stone. There are also kitchen and herb gardens, an orchard and soft fruit garden and a series of model gardens created to show visitors how to garden successfully in small urban areas. Further away from the house, a wisteria-clad bridge spanning the River Cray leads to lawns planted with ornamental trees, including a black poplar *Populus nigra* planted to commemorate Queen Elizabeth II's Diamond Jubilee in 2012.

Given Hall Place's success with Green Flag awards, it is no surprise to find wildlife areas within the garden, including ponds and a wildflower meadow. In the former walled garden there is a sub-tropical glasshouse with a collection of tender plants from around the world, including ripening bananas in mid-winter! Perhaps one of the most striking features in this garden is the Topiary Lawn, where a remarkable collection of ten yew-sculpted heraldic animals, known as The Queen's Beasts, were planted in 1953 to mark the coronation of Queen Elizabeth II.

The Topiary Lawn.

The Rose Gardens in full bloom.

❃ HAM HOUSE AND GARDEN

The National Trust has done such an excellent job in taking this Historic Grade II Listed geometric garden back to its seventeenth-century roots that its creators, Elizabeth Murray and the Duke of Lauderdale, would undoubtedly feel at home in its confines. However, one aspect which may puzzle them today is the preponderance of green parakeets which flock to the walnut and chestnut trees in the outer courtyard.

Built in 1610 alongside the River Thames, Ham House, with its avenues of lime trees striding out across Ham Common, was owned by Elizabeth Murray from the 1650s until her death in 1698. With her second husband, the Duke of Lauderdale, she spent much of her money and enthusiasm creating an impressive formal garden in keeping with the fashionable court of King Charles II. Its inspiration came from the Baroque gardens of Europe and in particular those in the Dutch style. In 1975 the National Trust reinstated its appearance by recreating Elizabeth's garden using documentary evidence and plans drawn up by John Slezer and Jan Wyck in 1671. Today, the garden is one of very few examples from that period that is still in existence.

Perhaps Ham's best known feature is the formal diamond-shaped parterre in the Cherry Garden. Here, clipped balls of glaucous-blue lavender and silver-grey santolina, sit like dusted chocolates in display cases created from box edging ▸

Ham House.

◀ punctuated with symmetrical box cones. The whole is bordered by tight-clipped yew hedging and perhaps best viewed from within the adjacent stilted walkway arches of clipped hornbeam.

Classical statuary abounds in this garden, including nearly forty busts of English kings and Roman emperors, positioned in niches in the weathered red-brick garden walls and flanked by drums of evergreen bay. Colour is added to the south-facing terrace below the house with regimental rows of terracotta urns, each holding an evergreen cone. The geometric patterns are carried through to the close-mown squares of grass, known as 'plats', each bisected by paths. In places the walls are softened by espaliered fruit including apples, pears, figs and vines. Beyond the walls lies The Wilderness, where more statuary and hornbeam hedges provide the setting for spring bulbs and native wild flowers. The Orangery, built in 1674 and draped in wisteria, is reputed to be the oldest in Britain and looks down upon terraces furnished with white-painted wooden planters containing olives and citrus. Work is continuing on the ornamental walled Kitchen Garden, which provides produce to the Orangery café.

The diamond-shaped parterre.

Classical statuary in the walled garden.

Stilted hornbeam and parterre.

❊ HAMPTON COURT PALACE GARDENS

Situated alongside the River Thames near East Molesey in Surrey, the gardens and grounds at Hampton Court Palace probably rank among the most famous in the world. Each year tens of thousands of visitors walk through them on their way to the Royal Horticultural Society's (and indeed the world's) biggest annual flower show, which straddles one of the gardens' main features – the Long Water Canal, excavated during the reign of Charles II in 1662. Outside the Flower Show period, Hampton Court Palace and its extensive gardens and grounds are constantly busy – an indication perhaps of a never-ceasing fascination with the history of the British monarchy as well as the beautiful and stunning garden landscapes found here.

King Henry VIII was the first monarch associated with Hampton Court, acquiring it from Cardinal Wolsey in the 1520s and extending and developing it in the grand style associated with palaces on the Continent. There are records of his Privy Gardens, which were laid out on the south side of the palace sometime between 1530 and 1538. Little if anything is left of that original garden, although a small knot garden planted in 1924 is said to replicate part of the sixteenth-century garden.

The bones of the present gardens and the wider landscape beyond were laid out in the late seventeenth century and were much influenced by the gardens at Versailles. Created on the ground by former pupils of Louis XIV's landscape gardener Andre Le Notre, their geometric design, tightly clipped yew and holly topiary and tree-lined avenues are typical of this period. Later ▶

Hampton Court maze.

❋ HAMPTON COURT PALACE GARDENS

◀ improvements in the Dutch Baroque-style were made to the garden during the reign of William & Mary (1689–1702) and include the Hampton Court maze, originally planted in hornbeam but repaired in places with yew and cypress and William III's 1702 Privy Garden, which has undergone restoration in recent years.

Today there are over 60 acres (24 hectares) of formal gardens, 750 acres (303 hectares) of royal parkland, 8,000 trees, the longest herbaceous border in Britain, a tender exotics collection and the Plant Heritage National Collection (NCCPG) of South American *Heliotropium arborescens;* all of which are managed and maintained by a team of thirty-eight gardeners, horticulturists and foresters. In the conservatory is the 'Great Vine', a Black Hamburg *Vitis vinifera* 'Schiava Grossa', reputedly planted by Lancelot 'Capability' Brown in 1768 and probably one of the oldest vines in the world still producing an annual crop of grapes.

The Privy Garden.

Influences from the garden at Versailles.

Bedding displays in the Privy Garden.

❁ THE HANNAH PESCHAR
SCULPTURE GARDEN

Set to a backdrop of beautiful luxuriant foliage, mature trees and tranquil pools, the Hannah Peschar Sculpture Garden is truly a garden like no other. Here, in a landscape that constantly changes from dappled light to shade, an inspirational ever-changing collection of sculpture (some of which is for sale) shows how human skill, endeavour, art and nature can come together in a celebration of both natural and human achievement. Shrubs, grasses, ferns and mature trees support, frame and enhance each individual piece, which reveal themselves sometimes gradually, sometimes with a dramatic sense of surprise, as one circumnavigates this atmospheric 10-acre (4-hectare) garden.

The range of works selected for display by owner/curator Hannah Peschar is wide, with styles varying from figurative to highly abstract, innovatively using a wide range of materials ranging from traditional stone, wood and bronze through to wire, glass, ceramic and plastic. Oriental themes play out where grey stepping stones lead across light-coloured gravel to a metal torso surmounted on a block of angular white stone, which contrasts so well against the ▶

Art and nature come together.

◀ rounded forms of nearby cloud-pruned pines. Elsewhere a black life-size stallion gazes across a pool, multicoloured botanical forms emerge from the water and glass bracket fungus grow upon a decaying tree trunk. Each sculpture is inspired by nature but, like a symbiotic relationship, each piece enhances the natural environment that surrounds it.

In the Victorian era the land formed part of the Leith Valley Estate and included a white-walled, timber-framed fifteenth-century Grade II Listed cottage, which remains to this day. The original garden was laid out around 1920, but eventually the estate was split up and sold off in several lots, one of which was a 10-acre (4-hectare) patch of the 1920s garden containing a stream, large pond and rock feature. By the time Hannah Peschar and her husband, landscape designer Anthony Paul, purchased the property in 1977, the garden had seen many years of neglect. Anthony and Hannah re-dug the pond and rerouted the stream, then beneath the canopy of the old estate trees began to create a new garden, planting in the process many native and exotic plants including grasses, bamboos, ligularias and other large-leaved plants, such as the ▶

The fifteenth-century Grade II listed cottage.

◀ architectural Chilean rhubarb *Gunnera manicata* which fringes the still green waters of three recently created ponds. In combination with natural woodland, elegant lawns and meandering streams the result is an inspired combination of peaceful enclosed harmony and sudden vistas set within an ever-changing environment.

One of the three recently created pools.

❈ HERSTMONCEUX CASTLE GARDENS

Situated in the East Sussex countryside, the delights of Herstmonceux begin as one obtains a first glimpse across ancient parkland, of its impressive red-brick fifteenth-century castle, which is one of the earliest brick buildings of significance still standing in England. The approach continues past the verdigris-domed science centre (also open to the public and particularly good for children), which was from 1957–88 home to the Royal Greenwich Observatory and beneath the remains of a 300-year-old sweet chestnut avenue, before running alongside the castle moat, which has recently had its banks cleared and boasts colourful displays of water lilies in summer.

Originally constructed as a grand country home and not for defensive purposes, the castle was in fact partially dismantled in 1777, leaving just the external walls standing. It remained an ivy-clad ruined folly until 1913 when then owner Col Lowther began a programme of restoration, which was completed by Sir Paul Latham in 1932. Today, Herstmonceux embodies the history and romance of medieval England and the Renaissance period, as well as hosting an international study centre for Queens University of Canada.

Herstmonceux's historic Grade II-Listed gardens are contained within a mixture of ancient walls dating back to before 1570 ▶

Herstmonceux Castle restored in 1932.

◀ and yew hedges, some of which have been clipped to mirror the castellated ramparts of the castle. Inside the walls and hedges there are a series of gardens. These include a paved herb garden with herbs growing in raised beds and a Shakespeare Garden with box parterre interplanted with lilies and *Gypsophila paniculata* and overlooked by fruit trees. There are also herbaceous borders complete with a diverse range of foxgloves *Digitalis* sp., daylilies *Hemerocaliis* sp. and *Nicotiana sylvestris* and rose gardens with single colour beds ranging from white through pink and orange to red and complemented by delightful sculpture.

Elsewhere there is an orchard which has been planted with old heritage varieties of fruit trees, a 'woodhenge', plantings of specimen Irish yew *Taxus baccata* 'Fastigiata' and an extensive woodland area. In all there are 550 acres (222 hectares) of woodland, parkland and gardens at Herstmonceux. Along the woodland trails there are significant collections of rhododendron dating from the Lowther/Latham period. The trails and walks also pass by a lily-covered lake, sculptures, waterfall and a Georgian-style folly built in the 1930s. In spring there are successional bulb displays from snowdrops, daffodils and bluebells, the latter being particularly delightful in early May when their hyacinth-like fragrance fills the air.

The Rose Garden.

Art within the garden.

❋ HEVER CASTLE GARDENS

This spectacular Grade I-Listed garden was laid out between 1904 and 1908 to a design drawn up by William Waldorf Astor. Over 1,000 workers were employed during its creation and 800 were involved in digging out the 35-acre (14-hectare) lake. Teams of horses transported mature trees from Ashdown Forest and steam engines moved rocks and soil to create 'natural' landscape features.

The garden, which is itself now part of Hever's history, surrounds and complements the double-moated thirteenth-century castle, which was once the home of Anne Boleyn. Sewn together in this way, they make for one of the most romantic landscapes in England.

Possibly the finest of the many garden features that Hever has to offer is the magnificent 4-acre (1.6-hectare) Italian Garden. Here long sweeping lawns, close-clipped yew hedging, shrubs and climbers both soften and accentuate exquisite and sometimes flamboyant hard landscaping, which includes pillared colonnades, broad curving steps flanked by stone balustrades, loggia, classical sculpture, statuary and stone and marble antiquities. Along the south side of the garden runs the Pergola Walk, which supports an array of camellias, wisteria, Virginia creeper and climbing roses. The walk fuses beautifully into the hillside beyond and in the process ▸

Chess topiary.

◀ produces a series of shaded grottoes, which are perfect for cool moisture-loving plants such as ferns, hostas, polygonums and astilbes.

For some it is Hever's quintessential English Rose Garden which is the highlight of their visit. Set within red-brick walls, it features more than 4,000 roses and from June until September is a sublime oasis of fragrance and colour. Planted formally in blocks of colour graduating from white, through pale pink and crimson to deep purple, it features hybrid teas, floribundas (including Hever's very own *Rosa* 'Horquinsey') and old-fashioned Alba and Bourbon varieties.

If this were not enough, Hever also boasts two mazes, one of water, situated on the aptly named Sixteen-Acre Island and planted with a range of aquatic plants, and a yew maze set close to the water-lily-covered outer moat and alongside the Tudor Garden, which shelters a series of smaller gardens, including a Chess Garden where the pieces are clipped out of golden yew, and a Herb Garden which grows plants that would have been familiar to Henry VIII and Anne Boleyn.

Add to this a 360-ft- (110-metres) long herbaceous border and less formal areas such as the Rhododendron Walk and Anne Boleyn's Orchard and you can begin to see why Hever's gardens are so much admired.

Spring bulbs by the moat.

Hever's quintessential English Rose Garden.

❋ HIGH BEECHES WOODLAND AND WATER GARDEN

This delightful West Sussex 27-acre (10.9-hectare) woodland and water garden was originally established in 1906 by Col Giles Loder, an accomplished and knowledgeable plantsman who also hailed from the same family that created the gardens at Wakehurst Place and Leonardslee. In 1966 the garden was acquired by Anne and Edward Boscawen who have continued managing and developing the garden with the same degree of knowledgeable horticulture and taste as their predecessors. Over the years the garden has been extended with sensitive thinning of the original woodland and underplanting with a range of rare and unusual exotic woody plants, some of them originals collected by Frank Kingdon-Ward and Ernest Wilson. Today High Beeches is probably one of the finest woodland gardens in the south-east of England and one that provides colour and interest from March through to November. Its strength lies in its informality and there are several different walks which, like Borde Hill's streams, meander through the grounds, down a valley and past a series of ponds.

The season starts with the flowering of a fine collection of camellias which are accompanied by beautiful drifts of narcissus and other bulbs and several magnolias, including the sumptuous *Magnolia* ▶

The Woodland garden.

Rhododendrons and azaleas in spring.

◀ *campbellii* which produces bright pink flowers the size of tea plates. Soon after, great swathes of bluebells cover the woodland floor and Borde Hill's extensive array of rhododendrons and sweetly scented deciduous azaleas come to the fore. By June it is the Loderi rhododendron hybrids on the 'Loderi Walk' which take centre stage. Renowned for their fragrance, perhaps the finest hybrid of all is 'Loderi King George'. Borde Hill is however not all about rhododendrons, far from it; there are excellent displays of flowering dogwoods *Cornus sp.*, and in spring one of the 'must-see sights' is the pocket-handkerchief tree *Davidia involucrata* in flower, its white hanging bracts quivering in the slightest breeze.

By late June Borde Hill's National Collection of Stewartia (NCCPG, Plant Heritage) are beginning to flower, their delightful camellia-like blooms always a curiosity for visitors, while nearby, an ancient acid wildflower meadow is awash with colour from wild orchids, cowslips and oxeye daisies. Summer highlights include *Hydrangea paniculata* 'Grandiflora' growing by Centre Pond and glades of *Gentiana asclepiadea,* the only naturalised site of willow gentian in the UK.

It almost goes without saying that with such a strong collection of woody plants the autumn is a blaze of brilliant leaf colours, but look out for carpets of Ivy-leaved cyclamen *Cyclamen hederifolium* too.

Hydrangea paniculata 'Grandiflora' by the Centre pond.

HOLE PARK GARDENS

Situated close to the picturesque Wealden village of Rolvendon on the Kent/Sussex border, Hole Park is a delightful red-brick and tiled early eighteenth-century country house, which was enlarged in 1830 but then reconstructed back to its earlier lines in 1959. Surrounding the house are 200 acres (81 hectares) of parkland dotted with wizened ancient oak and ash and bisected by a chestnut-lined drive.

The estate has been owned by the Barham family for the past four generations and it was Col Barham, the great grandfather of the present owner, who originally created the 15-acre (6-hectare) garden which surrounds the house in the years between the two world wars. Today, that same garden has matured into a truly magical landscape and one that is immaculately maintained throughout.

One of the great delights of Hole Park is that it is still relatively undiscovered, and unlike many of its better-known garden 'cousins' within the region, still manages to retain the peace and tranquillity that was once the trademark of the English country ▶

Japanese maples in the woodland gardens.

Bluebells in spring..

◀ house garden. Around the house, elegant garden rooms are sheltered by mellow red-brick walls and neatly trimmed yew hedging, which also acts as a backdrop to the many specimen plants to be found here. In places the yews themselves become the dominant features, having been clipped into strong geometric topiary shapes. The easy, sometimes seamless flow from formal to relaxed-style landscapes is one of Hole Park's great strengths, and Italianate terraces surfaced with golden-coloured gravel, statues and fountains are continually being softened by herbaceous borders and flowing lawns.

It is hard to imagine that the view from the main lawn across the lily pool, with its sentinel half-barrels of flowering Oxbridge-blue agapanthus, to the south façade of the house, has changed markedly since the garden's creation. In fact, such is the feeling of timelessness in this garden that if the colonel himself, in period military uniform, emerged from the shadows of the fine evergreen magnolia *Magnolia grandiflora* growing alongside the house, one would hardly raise an eyebrow.

In the semicircular Vineyard garden, a series of freestanding wisteria 'trees' make for a fine feature, while further away from the house formality gives way to meadows and sheltered woodland dells, through which a stream runs into shady pools fringed by marginal moisture-loving plants including giant-leaved Chilean rhubarb *Gunnera manicata*. Here, in spring, ornamental trees and shrubs and banks of rhododendrons and azaleas prolifically flower above an exquisite carpet of bluebells.

Free-standing Wisteria 'trees'.

❁ IGHTHAM MOTE

Situated in the Kentish Weald, Ightham Mote's 14-acre (5.6-hectare) garden surrounds a beautiful medieval and Tudor manor house with half-timbered walls and red-tiled roof, adorned by tall elegant chimneys. Both house and garden nestle in a sunken wooded valley, which also contains the stream that provides water for the moat around the house.

Water is an integral part of Ightham and the sight, or sound of it, is never far away. In the late eighteenth and early nineteenth centuries, a landscaped walk was created at the upper northern end of the garden. It included an ornamental lake and cascade, which has recently undergone restoration. The site of the main lawn was once a medieval stewpond used to provide fish for the dining table. Now the water which fed the stewpond flows in culverts beneath the lawn and straight into the moat from where it disgorges into a more recently created lake below.

There never was one great design plan for the garden at Ightham; it simply evolved over the centuries, in some cases as a response to changing fashions and requirements. In the Victorian era, naturalist Prideaux John Selby planted many exotic trees at Ightham. Sadly several of these succumbed to the Great Storm of October 1987, however to the south of the garden a magnificent London plane *Platanus* x *hispanica* managed to escape the storm and is surrounded by drifts of daffodils every spring. ▶

The Tudor manor house.

◀ The main ornamental garden lies to the west of the main lawn and house. A long border, full of grasses, perennials and shrubs, provides colour and interest throughout the growing season. Grasses such as *Miscanthus* sp. and *Stipa sp.* seem to do particularly well here and are perfect accompaniments to flowering *Gypsophila paniculata*, asters, geraniums and veronica.

The pool and fountain in Ightham's Formal Garden once formed part of an Italianate Garden. It later became a rose garden, but today is given over to gloriously exuberant displays of Victorian carpet bedding, which is designed and changed twice a year by Ightham's gardeners.

Enclosed within clipped yew hedging, the Cutting Garden is on the site of Victorian sunken glasshouses and is awash with colour throughout the spring and summer. It is at its best in June and July when the sweet pea and lavender walk fills the garden with fragrance. Nearby is The Orchard where heritage apple varieties and carpets of daffodils now grow on the site of the original sixteenth-century kitchen garden.

Ightham Mote from The Orchard.

The Long Border provides colour and interest throughout the year.

✤ KING JOHN'S NURSERY AND GARDEN

The romantic and atmospheric gardens of King John's Lodge are as beautiful as they are tranquil and have captured the hearts of many over the years. They surround a fine Grade II Listed, red-tile roofed 1650s Jacobean manor house, which is built on the site of an earlier building, as well as having later additions. Tucked away down winding country lanes amid the wooded hills of the High Weald in East Sussex and not far from the delightful village of Etchingham, the house takes its name from the belief that after the battle of Poitiers in 1356, John le Bon, the French King John II (1319–64), was taken prisoner by Edward the Black Prince and held captive here for a while.

The property was purchased by current owner Jill Cunningham and her late husband Richard in October 1987, shortly before the Great Storm. By the time they moved in they were faced with a garden and orchard strewn with scores of fallen trees. Over the following years they not only carried out an excellent restoration of the house but also rescued and redeveloped its 8-acre (3.2-hectare) plot. They first opened the garden under the National Gardens Scheme in the 1990s, then gradually more and more regularly ▸

Rustic charm.

❀ KING JOHN'S NURSERY AND GARDEN

◀ to the public. In 2006, on the site of two derelict chicken sheds, their eldest son Harry set up a plant nursery, with most of the stock being grown on site and this has since developed to include a shop and tearoom.

One of the great delights of the garden is that it not only has the romantic lines of the house as its backdrop but also some fine views out across grazing sheep and fluttering white fantail doves to picturesque parkland, which surrounds the southern and eastern sides of the house, and then beyond to the surrounding Sussex countryside.

Wisteria and rambling roses clothe the mellow-stone walls of the house and sun-loving perennials fill the terrace borders. There are formal lawns with a fountain and lily pond, and the original orchard, which still retains some of its old trees, has a series of mown paths which wind through meadow grass full of wild flowers. A particular favourite with visitors is a secret pond and woodland walk which features a statue of Oberon and Titania. The shady woodland is planted with hellebores, bulbs, ferns and foxgloves and by a natural pool and waterfall is a bog garden full of candelabra and drumstick primulas.

Secret ponds and woodland walks.

The gardens surround a Jacobean manor house.

✤ LULLINGSTONE CASTLE & THE WORLD GARDEN

Dating back to the time of Domesday and set within 120 acres (48.5 hectares) of beautiful Kent countryside, Lullingstone Castle is one of England's oldest family estates. The manor house and gate house, which overlook a stunning 15-acre (6-hectare) lake, were originally built in 1497 and have been home to the Hart Dyke family ever since. Both Henry VIII and Queen Anne are known to have been regular visitors to Lullingstone and hidden in the grounds, alongside the River Darent, are Queen Anne's bath house and an eighteenth-century ice house. Also in the grounds is St Botolph's parish church – delightful building of Norman origin containing some of England's oldest stained-glass windows. From 1932 until 1956 Lullingstone was also famous for its silk farm. Lullingstone silk was used within several royal garments including both the wedding dress and coronation robes of Her Majesty Queen Elizabeth II. ▶

The World Garden from the air.

✸ LULLINGSTONE CASTLE & THE WORLD GARDEN

◀ During 2005 and 2006 Tom Hart Dyke (twentieth generation of Hart Dykes to live at Lullingstone) created, within the Castle's 500-year-old 2-acre walled garden, a unique and beautiful 'World Garden of Plants' containing over 8,000 different plant species and varieties collected from all over the world. Tom's initial inspiration for the garden came in 2000 while on a plant-hunting expedition searching for orchids in Central America. During the expedition he was kidnapped at gunpoint and subsequently held hostage in the Columbian jungle for nine months.

On his release Tom recorded his experiences in a bestselling book entitled *The Cloud Garden*, and a BBC television documentary series followed the creation of the World Garden in 2005 and 2006.

In essence the garden pays homage to the amazing achievements of Victorian and Edwardian plant-hunters who risked life and limb in pursuit of the plants and flowers we now cherish and grow within our gardens in the UK. The beds take the form of the world's continents and the paths between them represent the oceans. As one travels through the garden it becomes apparent just how many of our common garden plants originate from foreign lands. For example, the North American beds contain poppies, lupins and Echinacea; 'Africa' is planted with agapanthus, montbretia and red-hot pokers; and within the Australasian beds there are pittosporums, hebes and olearias by the score.

The garden continues to grow year on year – Tom Hart Dyke's boundless enthusiasm sees to that – and in recent years an impressive collection of cacti and succulents have been added.

Lullingstone Castle.

The North American Beds.

❈ LOSELEY PARK

Set in the Surrey Hills Area of Outstanding Natural Beauty (AONB), the Loseley estate covers 1,400 acres (566 hectares) and has been home to the More-Molyneux family for over 500 years. At its centre sits an Elizabethan manor house, built in the 1560s, containing original panelling from Henry VIII's Nonsuch Palace.

Loseley's extensive walled garden was originally laid out in the sixteenth century and is not immediately obvious on arrival. It is in fact hidden behind an archway to the east of the house. Originally a functional garden producing fruit, vegetables and cut flowers, there have been many changes over the years, including the creation of herbaceous borders designed by Gertrude Jekyll. Her original borders no longer exist, however borders on the north wall today reflect the structure and planting she would have used. Close by is a magnificent ancient wisteria which has been underplanted with purple irises, both of which flower at their best in May and early June. On the lawn near the entrance another ancient plant survives – a prostrate black mulberry tree *Morus nigra* reputed to have been planted by Queen Elizabeth I.

In all, the walled garden is comprised of five main gardens each with its own theme and character. There is an enchanting, award-winning rose garden planted with over 1,000 rose bushes, mainly old-fashioned varieties including bourbons, gallicas and rugosas, all framed by low box hedges. At its centre is a gazebo covered with creamy-white flowers of the Albert Barbier rose. Running alongside the rose garden is an arcade of purple-leaved vines and clematis. At the eastern end of the rose garden and beyond hedges of yew, is a herb garden divided into four 'usage' ▸

September-flowering kniphofias.

The Flower Garden.

The White Garden.

◂ sections: culinary, medicinal, household and ornamental.

Golden-fruited malus (crab apples) form a square avenue in the flower garden, which is designed to provide interest and bold fiery colour throughout the season and is particularly vibrant in early September with flowering kniphofias, heleniums and rudbeckias.

In total contrast, the nearby white garden is comprised of white, cream and silver plants, surrounding a rectangular lily pool with fountain and overseen by a resident population of white doves. The overall effect is both tranquil and sublime. An organic vegetable and cut-flower garden provides a nod back to the sixteenth century, and beyond the moat, which runs almost the entire length of the walled garden, is a wild-flower meadow planted on what used to be the Loseley cricket pitch.

Late summer colour.

❋ MARLE PLACE

Marle Place is a delightful, privately owned (open by appointment) 10-acre (4-hectare) garden surrounding a seventeenth-century house, tucked away up a quiet Kentish country lane. The name 'marle' refers to the crumbly, calcium-rich deposits found in the area, which in centuries past were used for soil enrichment. Marle Place owners, Gerald and Lindel Williams, one a plantsman and the other an artist, have used this favourable soil and their individual talents, to create layers of horticultural and artistic enhancement over a garden which was originally created in 1890. Sadly Gerald passed away in 2015, but Lindel continues to manage and maintain the garden.

Early garden features remaining include a Victorian gazebo, Edwardian rockery and an attractive Italianate fragrant walled garden laid out in 1900. There is also an excellent orchid collection housed in a beautifully restored nineteenth-century greenhouse, which is set within a yew-hedged potager kitchen garden that also contains a box parterre and a raised-bed rose garden.

The present garden has been designed as a collection of hedged rooms and tree-lined avenues. It is set on a southeast-facing slope and includes a 5-acre (2-hectare) arboretum, carpeted in summer with drifts of buttercups and clover and full of interesting, exotic and ornamental trees. Bordering the arboretum is a small stream, beyond which are acres of ▶

A collection of hedged rooms.

◀ orchards and Wealden woodland, typical of that found in the 'garden of England'.

Close to the house is a border of cistus, an old wall covered with unusual climbers including *Clianthus puniceus* and a small, cool, shady fern garden. Herbaceous and annual plants, in combination with shrubs and trees, provide scent, colour and interest from March through until autumn. In spring it is bulbs and blossom which predominate, followed in summer by old-fashioned roses and scented, flamboyant borders. Then from September it is foliage colours of the arboretum which take centre stage.

Other features include statuary, bamboo, a pasture of alliums and a bog garden with large-leaved foliage plants such as *Gunnera manicata* which is accessed across a vermillion-painted Chinese bridge. Water adds a further dimension to the garden, which has won several awards for wildlife management. Perhaps one of the more unusual features, and one that highlights the artistic talent of the owner, is a beautiful mosaic terrace set within a blue and yellow border. Other forms of artwork can be found throughout the garden and there is a gallery on site which exhibits work by contemporary artists.

Art is never far away in this garden.

The Victorian Gazebo.

❀ MOUNT EPHRAIM GARDENS

Located within the heart of Kent, Mount Ephraim is an atmospheric, privately owned, 800-acre (323-hectare) country estate. At its centre is a fine red-brick house, built in the latter part of the nineteenth century by Sir Edwin Dawes, a wealthy shipping importer. Surrounding the house are 10 acres (4 hectares) of timeless, Edwardian-influenced, terraced gardens. As both house and gardens are situated in an elevated position, there are far-reaching views across fruit orchards towards the Thames Estuary and on a clear day, to the Essex coastline beyond.

Home to the Dawes family for over 300 years, much of the present garden was laid out in the early 1900s, but by the end of the Second World War it was in a neglected state. From the 1950s Mary and Bill Dawes began a restoration programme and Mary had active involvement in the garden until her death in 2009. Today her daughter-in-law Lesley continues to restore and develop the garden with the help of two full-time gardeners, plus some part-time and volunteer assistance.

The house overlooks sweeping lawns, huge borders and magnificent specimen trees, including a sweet chestnut planted to commemorate the Battle of Waterloo. The steeply sloping site retains the original formal plan of the rose terrace, with flights of steps hedged by yew leading to a tranquil lake and water garden. ▶

The rock and water garden.

❈ MOUNT EPHRAIM GARDENS

◀ The restored Japanese-influenced rock and water garden includes Japanese lanterns and several pools, crossed by a Japanese stone bridge.

Perhaps some of the finest features at Mount Ephraim are found in the topiary garden where an eclectic collection of birds, animals and First World War memorabilia has been fashioned out of clipped yew. A long herbaceous border, skilfully planted and sheltered by old stable walls, lines the topiary garden and provides colour throughout the summer. Beyond the topiary garden is a delightful rose garden created for the millennium and planted with fragrant new and old-fashioned roses which ramble and scramble over wrought-iron arches and an arbour. The garden also includes a 'Mizmaze' – a medieval-style turf labyrinth which is flanked by ornamental grasses, herbaceous perennials and wild flowers to give a meadow effect, and is seen at its best towards the end of summer.

Mount Ephraim is also home to an extensive collection of spring bulbs, trees and shrubs, including rhododendrons, camellias and magnolias.

A small arboretum was planted in 1995 to commemorate both Mary Dawes' eightieth birthday and the 300th anniversary of the Dawes family's association with Mount Ephraim.

The topiary garden.

❁ MERRIMENTS

The owners of this impressive 4-acre (1.6-hectare) Sussex garden, David and Peggy Weeks, are intelligent and knowledgeable gardeners and it shows, both in their choice and placing of plants and in the high level of maintenance found throughout the garden. Many of the plants here are unusual and quite often found in the neighbouring nursery of the same name.

Although not an old garden, it was only developed from an open field in the 1990s, Merriments already has the feel of a well-established plot with a character and atmosphere that is normally associated with much older gardens. Part of this is simply down to good gardening, ensuring each plant is given the right conditions to keep it healthy and growing vigorously; this is particularly obvious with the many clematis and roses in the garden. Thoughtful and densely planted partnerships of herbaceous perennials, ornamental grasses, roses and shrubs, sometimes underplanted with tulips, alliums and hostas, provide screens that separate out each meandering border and island bed and create a level of intimacy that both absorbs people and makes the garden feel much larger than it actually is. ▶

Developed from an open field in the 1990s.

◄ Throughout the garden the labelling is good and the planting deliberately chosen to provide a long season of colour, texture and fragrance. In truth there are ideas to steal here aplenty with imaginative plant combinations for every situation, from a shady bog garden filled with moisture-loving lush marginals to a sunbaked Blue Gravel Garden with Agapanthus sp. and *Verbena bonariensis*. Vibrant warm colours abound in the Golden Border, which is at its best in late summer.

The large-leaved tropical plantings around the two ponds, which are crossed by a striking bridge built in 2004, is the perfect alternative to the busy herbaceous borders, and in late spring the linking dry stream bed is full of flowering candelabra primulas and drifts of alliums.

More recently a new entrance garden has been created in the style of Monet's Grande Allee at Giverny, but this is just one in a whole series of features which will both inspire and delight within this beautiful garden. There is a walled formal garden with rill, a glade of silver birch underplanted with crocus and wood anemones, a wild garden with meadow and bird-hide, fine golden-foliaged specimen trees such as *Gleditsia triancanthos* 'Sunburst' and *Catalpa bignonioides* 'Aurea' and benches, arbours, summerhouses, pergolas, pagodas and large terracotta pots all providing a series of focal points around the garden.

Pergolas add height to the borders.

Early autumn glow.

Plant combinations for every situation.

❀ NYMANS

Originally created by wealthy stockbroker Ludwig Messel and his notable head gardener James Comber from the 1860s onwards, the gardens at Nymans were further expanded and developed by Ludwig's son Leonard and then by his granddaughter Anne, Countess of Rosse, before being given to the National Trust in 1954. Today the garden is rightly considered to contain one of the finest woody plant collections in England and includes many original introductions, some collected in the wild by James Comber's son Harold as well as approximately forty home-bred varieties. Within the latter, two gems shine out: *Magnolia x loebneri* 'Leonard Messel', which produces beautiful star-shaped pink flowers in April, and *Eucryphia x nymansensis* 'Nymansay', a stunning tall summer-flowering shrub that fills the air with sweet fragrance accompanied by the soporific drone of nectar-collecting bees in August and September.

The collection covers almost the entire 30-acre (12-hectare) site, but it is beautifully structured and set within a multitude of garden landscapes including flowing serpentine-edged lawns, island beds, garden 'rooms' contained by evergreen hedges and well-maintained borders. Despite the breadth of the collection, the garden does not feel overcrowded and there is all important space to stand back and enjoy the form and positioning of each individual plant. This is perhaps not entirely due to intelligent foresight by the family and latterly the National Trust, as the Great Storm of 1987 did much to weed out overmature specimens and open up vistas. Nonetheless it is good to see that the Trust has resisted the temptation to fill every gap with young plants. ▸

The Summer Borders.

◀ The original Messel features still in existence include a pinetum, a sunken garden with stone loggia bedecked in wisteria, a laurel walk, a rose garden, a walled garden and magnificent herbaceous borders – which are full of colour from June until October. In recent years Messel's extensive heather garden and rockery has been completely revamped and is establishing well, as can be seen from the mound above the croquet lawn. Japanese influences within this part of the garden include stone lanterns acquired from the Japan-British Exhibition of 1910 and a recently planted collection of 'Wilson's Fifty', a collection of Kurume azaleas selected by the plant collector in Japan in 1918. A modern nod in the direction of this great man can be found in the young grove of his most famous plant introduction, the pocket handkerchief tree *Davidia involucrata,* recently planted by Alastair Buchanan, a descendent of Ludwig Messel.

The burnt-out shell of the house.

One of the spring borders.

Giant Pieris date back to the Messel period.

❀ PAINSHILL LANDSCAPE GARDEN

This magnificent, authentically restored, 158-acre (64-hectare) eighteenth-century landscape garden was laid out between 1738 and 1773 by The Hon. Charles Hamilton. Created as a romantic landscape to 'stimulate the emotions', it is divided into two distinct areas: ornamental pleasure grounds including a 14-acre (5.6-hectare) serpentine lake and adjoining open parkland laid out in a 'free and natural style' with strategic clumps of trees used in Lancelot 'Capability' Brown fashion.

Contemporary with Stowe and Stourhead, Painshill is today regarded as one of the most important landscape parks of its type in Britain and holds Historic Garden Grade I Listing.

Despite several changes of ownership, Painshill was well maintained until World War II, but then sold off in lots in 1948 and almost lost. However between 1974 and 1980 Elmbridge Council bought up the majority of the land and in 1981 the Painshill Park Trust was set up and began the task of restoration with initial support from the National Heritage Memorial Fund.

Today restoration is still ongoing, but much has been done since 1981 and a ▸

Across the lake to the Gothic Temple.

◀ visit to Painshill is both a fascinating and enjoyable experience.

While the contrived rolling land formations are clever in their execution, it is the water features and follies which catch the eye, as indeed they are supposed to, revealed one by one as visitors promenade the park. Firstly the eastern end of the lake is revealed, it's curving form and positioning of islands ensuring it is not seen in its entirety and so the viewer is deceived as to its actual size. On its banks, a Gothic Ruined Abbey built in 1772, is deliberately placed so that its front façade reflects off the still water, the effect is truly sublime but in truth just a taste of what is to come. A wooden, white painted Chinese Bridge, restored in 1988, leads to the Grotto Islands, clad with fine Cedar of Lebanon trees and linked by an artificial series of chambers complete with stalactites and pools. At the far end of the lake is the Turkish Tent, originally built in 1760 but lost long ago, drawings from the period have allowed for its recreation and it once again offers magnificent vistas back across the lake to the Gothic Temple, perfectly positioned in a glade surrounded by informal plantings of shrubs and trees. Productive walled gardens, a vineyard and a fine collection of North American trees and shrubs add further interest to this remarkable garden.

The Turkish Tent.

The Gothic Temple.

The Ruined Abbey.

✵ PARHAM HOUSE

Set in the heart of an 875-acre (354-hectare) medieval deer park, still grazed today by a dark form of fallow deer descended from the original herd recorded in 1628, Parham House has been described as one of England's finest surviving examples of an Elizabethan manor house.

West of the house lies Parham's Historic Grade II Listed 7-acre (2.8-hectare) pleasure grounds, originally laid out in the eighteenth century. Here, early introductions of exotic trees, a grove of 'Shirotae' Japanese flowering cherries, a peaceful lake overlooked by Cannock House (a classical summer house which has recently undergone restoration), a belvedere, a further three-arched summer house, a glade of recently planted magnolias including *Magnolia* 'Yellow Fever' and a quarter-of-a-mile-long brick and turf maze, created in 1991 to celebrate 'The Year of the Maze' and inspired by the design on a sixteenth-century embroidery, all ensure that garden lovers will be more than satisfied by their visit. However, this is just one part of Parham's horticultural offering, for to the north of the house lies one of the loveliest walled gardens in England and a past winner of the prestigious HHA/Christies Garden of the Year Award to boot.

Approached through *Actinidia chinensis*-clad wrought-iron gates guarded by a pair of Istrian stone lions, the 4-acre (1.6-hectare) walled garden is believed to predate the house and was cultivated in the fourteenth century by monks from the monastery of Westminster. Exactly what was grown at that time is uncertain, ▶

Borders near the garden entrance.

◀ but as the name 'Parham' means 'Pear Enclosure', it is quite likely that fruit played a part. In more recent years the garden has been divided into four distinct areas, based on the original quadrant layout with an emphasis more towards ornamental rather than productive planting, although vegetables are grown within an elegant parterre and an orchard has recently been re-established with traditional varieties of dessert apples including 'Lord Lambourne', 'Sturmer Pippin' and 'Newton Wonder'.

Elsewhere it is a garden of mixed borders, some full to overflowing with Edwardian-style floriferous exuberance, others tranquil and calming through the clever use of prairie-style plantings of *Calamagrostis x acutifolia* 'Karl Foerster' and *Deschampsia cespitosa*. There is also a yew-enclosed herb garden surrounding a pond, complete with cherub, a rose ▶

Across the walled garden to the house.

◀ and lavender garden which uses blooms of pastel colours in combination with glaucous-grey foliage and in complete contrast, an exotic garden of bright bold colours, bamboos and dramatic large-leaved foliage. Individually each garden is a delight; collectively the result is a triumph.

Parham House.

✤ PASHLEY MANOR

Pashley Manor, the family home of Mr and Mrs James Sellick since 1981, is situated deep within the quintessentially English and leafy borderland of Kent and Sussex. It is a beautiful Grade I Listed Tudor timber-framed former ironmaster's house dating from 1550 with Georgian enlargements from 1720. Surrounding the property is a 10-acre (4-hectare) garden, which has not only been called 'one of the finest gardens in England' but is also a past recipient of the prestigious HHA/Christie's Garden of the Year Award.

Here you will see romantic English landscaping and artistic, imaginative planting framed by fine old trees and mellow red-brick walls, enhanced by fountains and ponds and all to the backdrop of rolling Home Counties countryside glimpsed from terrace and through sublime wrought ironwork.

The garden was first opened to the public by the Sellicks in 1992 following renovation and assistance from the eminent landscape architect, the late Anthony du Gard Pasley. Almost twenty-five years later the garden retains its original integrity, with high standards of maintenance and subtle use of colour and form. Perhaps some of the best examples of this can be seen in the ▶

Perfectly placed sculpture.

◀ borders which grow on the outside of the eighteenth-century walled garden, including a particularly successful 'hot border' with bright red roses and Inca lilies *Alstroemeria sp* set against a foil of purple-leaved cotinus interwoven with golden-yellow day lilies *Hemerocallis sp.*

Although this is a three-season garden (and the Tulip Festival in late April is not to be missed), it is perhaps in summer that Pashley really comes into its own. In June and early July the garden overflows with colour from more than 100 varieties of rose, repeatedly planted. While concentrated within the walled garden, they are to be found throughout Pashley, sometimes individually as with the pure yellow, wall-trained climber Rosa 'Graham Thomas' and sometimes in swathes of palest pink skirting an elegantly sculpted female form. There is delightful sculpture and art strategically placed throughout the garden, some in dominant positions on the lawns which sweep down from the house and Garden Room café to a series of ponds and fountain and others enchantingly placed in sylvan isolation alongside woodland paths which circumnavigate the old moat.

On hot sunny days you will undoubtedly migrate to the swimming pool garden, ▶

The eighteenth-century walled garden.

◀ where you can immerse yourself in a fine collection of succulents and Mediterranean plantings before entering Pashley's Victorian greenhouse bedecked with fragrant and interesting climbers including jasmine, loquat and passiflora.

The Rose Garden.

❊ PENSHURST PLACE

Originally built in 1341, Penshurst Place has been described as 'the most perfectly preserved example of a fortified manor house in all of England'. It has been the home of the Sidney family since 1552. Surrounding the house are 48 acres (19 hectares) of grounds, including 11 acres (4.5 hectares) of Historic Grade I Listed gardens, some of which are as old as the house, with terraces and walls providing the backdrop to a series of garden 'rooms' which date back to the Elizabethan era. Much of the original garden has undergone restoration by the present owner, his father and his grandfather. One of the latest projects in the ongoing restoration programme has been the 240-ft- (73-metre) long double herbaceous borders, replanted to a design by RHS Chelsea Gold Medallist George Carter. Renamed the Jubilee Walk in 2012, it includes stone benches set into the borders, heritage varieties of apple trees and colour coordinated plantings of both herbaceous material and shrubs.

Each garden room, bordered by over 1 mile (1.6 kms) of close-clipped yew hedging, offers a different theme and collectively provide colour and interest from spring to autumn. Close to the entrance is a garden for those with impaired vision, with tactile ▸

Garden rooms date back to the Elizabethan era.

◀ and aromatic plants growing in raised beds, a wooden gazebo and a small fountain where water can be heard splashing onto pebbles. To the south front of the house is an Italianate garden laid out with symmetrical bedding schemes bordered by low box hedging and an oval-shaped lily pool fountain with a classical statue at its centre. Nearby on the south lawn, with its beds of lavender and roses, stands a fine century-old *Ginkgo biloba*, otherwise known as the maidenhair tree because of its curiously shaped leaves, which are similar to the maidenhair fern.

Beyond the mellow-stoned garden tower is a striking blue and yellow border, designed using the colours of the Sidney family coat of arms. Restored in 2013, it now contains specially bred Penshurst irises in both colours. Keeping with the family theme, in the Heraldic Garden and rising from a parterre of box, lavender and sage are brightly coloured knightly poles topped with Sidney heraldic animals.

Other features to enjoy include double mixed borders created in 1970 by American garden designer Lanning Roper with a fine westerly vista towards Penshurst Church, a beautiful Rose Garden bordered by purple-leaved berberis, a magnolia garden, sliver and white garden, orchard, and two medieval stew ponds.

The Italianate Garden.

✺ PETWORTH HOUSE

L ocated on the edge of the attractive Sussex market town from which it takes its name, this stately mansion has one of the finest late seventeenth-century house interiors in England.

It sits within 700 acres (283 hectares) of rolling parkland originally landscaped by Lancelot 'Capability' Brown. Considered to be one of Brown's finest achievements, and painted by both Turner and Constable, the park is comprised of sweeping grassland, a serpentine lake, a herd of around 900 fallow deer and perfectly placed groupings of trees – primarily oak, beech, sweet chestnut and sycamore. A significant number of the original trees were destroyed by the Great Storm of

October 1987 and since then the National Trust, who were given Petworth by the 3rd Lord Leconfield in 1947, have done much to restore and replant both at the head of the lake and throughout the park and its associated Pleasure Grounds. To date close on 50,000 young trees have been planted and already the earliest ones are making a significant contribution to the landscape. In places some original trees remain, stag-headed, twisted and full of character. These venerable veterans, now almost 270 years old, bear witness to the passing of time and look out across Petworth's 14-mile (22.5-km) stonewalled boundary onto a very different world to the one they were planted into. ▶

Daffodils in the park.

◀ The Pleasure Grounds lie to the north of the house and were also worked on by 'Capability' Brown. Bordered by a ha-ha and extending to 30 acres (12 hectares), they are best described as a woodland garden with eye-catchers, which includes a fine Doric Temple set amid groves of ornamental trees including *Acer palmatum* and *Acer rubrum* 'October Glory', which, as the name suggests, produces stunning leaf colour in autumn.

In spring the grounds burst into life with displays of primroses and Lent lilies *Narcissus pseudonarcissus*. These are followed by swathes of bluebells, orchids, fritillaries and camassias, all of which flower alongside significant collections of rhododendrons and other spring-flowering shrubs. On the slopes surrounding an eighteenth century Ionic Rotunda there are fine groupings of deciduous fragrant rhododendrons including *Rhododendron* 'Narcissiflorum', *R. luteum*, *R. palestrina* and *R. visicosum*.

The walk from the National Trust car park and visitor centre (just off the A283 Guildford road) to Petworth House, takes ten to fifteen minutes at a leisurely stroll and passes through ornamental collections of trees including North American oaks, tulip trees and limes and past island beds full to overflowing with shrub roses, hydrangeas, laurels and dogwoods.

The Ionic Rotunda.

Drifts of daffodils in front of the Doric Temple.

❋ POLESDEN LACEY

There are historic references to this Grade II Listed Historic Garden going back to 1333, but it is for the Edwardian gardens, created by society hostess Mrs Greville, that visitors flock to Polesden Lacey today. In truth, they come first and foremost to capture a glimpse of high society in those seemingly carefree early twentieth-century years before dark war clouds began to gather across Europe.

Mrs Greville purchased Polesden Lacey in 1906 (she was the daughter of Scottish brewery multi-millionaire William McEwan)

and immediately began to transform it into a house fit to host lavish parties. In June 1909 she hosted her first official house party with King Edward VII as the guest of honour. He was already a regular house guest having planted a mulberry in the grounds on his first visit on 19 May 1907. For nearly four decades the parties flowed and prime ministers, princes, maharajahs, ambassadors and captains of industry enjoyed Mrs Greville's hospitality – George VI and Queen Elizabeth the Queen Mother even had their honeymoon here. Polesden ▶

Royal visitors.

Recently restored herbaceous borders.

The Garden Cottage.

◀ Lacey became the Ritz of the countryside and oh what countryside, its high downland setting in the Surrey hills with magnificent views to the south across some 940 acres (380 hectares) of woodland and farmland made the perfect backdrop to Mrs Greville's 30-acre (12-hectare) garden.

It was a garden very much of its time, a blend of open lawns, mature native and exotic trees, formal terraces and elaborate rose gardens, quartered by stone-flagged paths fringed by lavender, above which timber pergolas played host to a multitude of climbing roses. Today, although some of the planting may have changed, the structure is much as it was a century ago and from a deckchair on the South Lawn you can still gaze across the Surrey hills, although several of the original trees were blown down in the Great Storm of October 1987.

To the west of the house, in a peaceful small enclosure surrounded by yew hedging, is the grave of Mrs Greville, watched over by four statues depicting the four seasons. Beyond lies the walled Rose Garden and inside, the four large rectangular rose beds are still given over to Edwardian soft pastel colours, while the borders against the weathered red-brick walls are full of interesting flowering shrubs. Recently restored colourful herbaceous borders, gardens of lavender and irises and a delightful cut-flower garden all add to the enjoyment of this period masterpiece.

The Cut-flower Garden.

❀ RAMSTER

The gardens at Ramster were first laid out in 1890 by Gauntletts nursery of Chiddingfold in oak woodland to the side of Ramster's attractive seventeenth-century red-brick manor house (not regularly open to the public).

Gauntletts were well known for their interest and expertise in the design of Japanese-style gardens, which were considered fashionable in Britain during a period lasting from the latter part of the Victorian era through until the First World War. Stone lanterns, cranes feeding in the ponds, large clumps of bamboos, massed plantings of evergreen azaleas and a fine double row of Japanese maples *Acer palmatum* 'Atropurpureum Dissectum' all remain in the garden from that period.

Ramster was purchased by Sir Henry and Lady Norman in 1922 and has been owned by the same family ever since. Lady Norman grew up at Bodnant on the edge of the Snowdonia National Park and many of the stunning rhododendrons and azaleas, some over 65 feet (20 metres) tall, which flourish beneath Ramster's mature woodland canopy today, originate from the Aberconway rhododendron collection at Bodnant. Some were grown from seed brought back by plant-collectors such as George Forrest and Frank Kingdon-Ward and others were the result of hybridisation by Lady Norman herself. The soil at ▶

Rhododendron bower.

◀ Ramster ranges from acid to neutral, primarily Wealden clay interspersed with pockets of sand, making it ideal for the growing of rhododendrons, camellias, magnolias and azaleas.

Today, the garden covers 20 acres (8 hectares) and includes a pond and lake, a collection of over 200 recently planted hybrid azaleas, a bog garden and rill planted in 1998 with candelabra primulas and giant-leaved gunnera *Gunnera manicata,* a paved Millennium Garden on the site of an old tennis court and a number of sculptures including a delightful grouping of young children playing, perfectly positioned in the centre of an informal lawn surrounded by rhododendrons, azaleas and other spring-flowering shrubs.

Despite these new additions Ramster has managed to retain a natural unspoilt character with winding grass paths leading to tranquil woodland glades overhung by floriferous bowers. In spring the ground is alive with wild flowers, narcissi and carpets of bluebells, which fill the air with a heady hyacinth-like fragrance. The warmth of June brings forth Mediterranean grasses and the subtle pink flowers of climbing roses.

Wildlife abounds throughout the garden and kingfishers, herons, ducks, geese and moorhens can frequently be seen around the lake and pond.

Sublime sculpture.

Spring at Ramster.

✤ RHS GARDEN WISLEY

In 1903, Sir Thomas Hanbury, a wealthy Quaker and creator of La Mortola garden on the Italian Riviera, presented the Royal Horticultural Society with 60 acres (24 hectares) of freehold land at Wisley, which included a garden previously known as 'Oakwood', located roughly where the RHS Wild Garden is today. By May 1904 the RHS had moved from their previous garden adjoining Chiswick House to Wisley and within a year were constructing a range of glasshouses. Sadly these were demolished in 1969 and the earliest RHS Wisley feature surviving to this day is the Rock Garden, which was completed in 1911.

Today the RHS garden at Wisley extends to more than 200 acres (81 hectares) and is regarded throughout the world as a centre of excellence for not only horticulture but horticultural education and new plant trials too. Wisley's plant collection is one of the largest in the world, encompassing around 30,000 different taxa, and what makes it so unique is its diversity. Where else on one site would you find such well-managed and well-labelled comprehensive collections of vegetables, fruit, alpines, tropica plants, succulents, waterlilies, cacti, orchids, bulbs, annuals, herbaceous, shrubs, climbers and trees? ▸

Autumn at Wisley.

◀ There is however much more to Wisley than just its plant collections. It is also a garden for people, a garden that will delight, educate and inspire no matter when you visit, be it the depths of winter when frosted-ice sparkles on sulphur-yellow witch hazel blooms, or the height of summer when the trial fields are a blaze with paint-box regimental patterns.

Having said all of this, it would be easy to forget the obvious and that is Wisley is also a beautiful landscape, or more accurately a series of beautiful landscapes, which begin immediately on entering the ornate wrought-iron-worked Wilks Gates displaying the date of the Society's founding in 1804. From here, with back turned to the half-timbered, red-tiled laboratory, the vista along Jellicoe's Canal to the Loggia beyond, bedecked in *Wisteria floribunda,* is quite simply sublime and includes one of the largest collections of waterlilies (*Nymphaea*) on one stretch of water in the UK. Add to this walled gardens, sweeping lawns spotted with majestic conifers, lakes with marginal bog plants, free-flowing Piet Oudolf borders, a rose garden, a bonsai collection, heather banks, a woodland garden, collections of rhododendron, camellia, magnolia and azalea sweeping across Battleston Hill, an arboretum, model gardens and glasshouses and you will begin to understand why Wisley is held in such high regard.

Near Battleston Hill.

The Rock Garden.

Spring bulb displays.

❀ RIVERHILL HIMALAYAN GARDENS

Originally built in 1714 on the site of a Tudor farm, the Riverhill House estate was purchased in 1840 by keen horticulturist and contemporary of Charles Darwin, John Rogers. It is said that Rogers purchased the property because of its tracts of acid soil, south-facing aspect and sheltered location. Records dating from 1842 show that soon after coming to Riverhill he began to establish a plantsmen's collection of trees and shrubs, including cedar of Lebanon trees and rhododendrons and azaleas underplanted with bulbs. Rogers was an early member of the Royal Horticultural Society and supported several overseas plant-hunting expeditions.

A second wave of planting took place around 1910 when Col John Middleton Rogers, aided by eight full-time gardeners, created what is now known as 'The Wood Garden', where, among other things, he planted a fine collection of Japanese maples, while his wife Muriel created a rock garden. Since then both the house and garden have gone through periods of neglect followed by renaissance. Today, the property still remains in the private ownership of the Rogers family and the passion for plants and gardening displayed by John Rogers over 175 years ago has passed down through the generations to current owners Edward and Sarah Rogers, who not only maintain the status quo, but since 2010 have been actively working on a restoration and renovation project. In that year they constructed a new car park for visitors, renovated the café, planted ▸

Alliums fringe the borders.

◂ a maze and began work on an adventure playground for children.

In 2011 the Rose Walk was restored and a full-time head gardener appointed. In 2012 the Walled Garden was re-landscaped and in 2013 the Riverhill maze was replanted with hornbeam, but this is only part of the story and a visit to Riverhill is a must for anyone who is interested in seeing how the old and the new can be perfectly blended within one historic landscape.

In the Walled Garden, once a productive area full of glasshouses growing melons, bananas and pineapples, there are Himalayan-inspired grass-sculpted terraces, a huge pond with fountains, swathes of summer-flowering displays and a formal productive vegetable garden. The nearby Rose Walk has beds filled with different varieties of roses deliberately chosen for repeat flowering right through the summer. In spring The Wood Garden boasts carpets of primroses and bluebells, topped by a vast number of rhododendrons and azaleas, which are at their best in May and June.

Blending the old and the new.

Plants collected from around the world.

Rhododendrons in the Himalayan Garden.

✤ THE SAVILL GARDEN WINDSOR

Savill Garden takes its name from Eric Humphrey Savill who was initially appointed Deputy Surveyor of the Royal Estate at Windsor Great Park in 1931 and then 'Keeper of the Gardens' during the reigns of both King George V and VI. Prior to Savill's appointment there was no public garden within Windsor Great Park at all. So, in 1932 he requested a small gardening budget and an area of land on which to create a garden. With the permission of King George V he chose an undulating site, through which a small stream ran on the south-eastern boundary of the park. His aim was to establish an ornamental woodland garden designed to be aesthetically pleasing to the eye and a joy to walk through.

Work began on the garden in the winter of 1932 and by 1934, when King George V and Queen Mary paid their first visit, the stream had been turned into a series of decorative ponds and the garden was planted with exotic trees, ornamental shrubs and flowering herbaceous plants originating from across the temperate world. Such was the success of the Royal visit that Savill was immediately allowed to expand the garden to its present 35 acres (14 hectares) and in ▸

The Golden Jubilee Garden.

The contemporary water fountain.

❀ THE SAVILL GARDEN WINDSOR

◀ the process set in motion a programme of planting which would lead to its future as one of Britain's finest ornamental gardens. In 1951 King George VI asked for the garden to be called 'The Savill Garden' and in 1955 Eric Savill was honoured with a knighthood.

Today, the Savill Gardens continue to develop and excel. In spring, the appropriately named Spring Wood is full of flowering rhododendrons, camellias and azaleas, complemented by swathes of narcissi, while fritillaries and sulphur-yellow spathes of American skunk cabbage *Lysichiton americanus* light up the marshy ground alongside the stream. In summer it is Savill's spectacularly colourful double

herbaceous borders and the Golden Jubilee Garden, opened by Her Majesty the Queen in 2002 to celebrate fifty years of her reign, which command attention. Here, a tranquil cottage-style design comprised of curving borders filled with swathes of pastel-shaded flowers surround a contemporary water feature, and if that were not enough, the Rose Garden with its innovative design and roses specially chosen for their scent and repeat flowering, is sure to please. Autumn brings intense leaf colours from scores of Japanese maples and in winter there are dogwoods, willows and trees with attractive bark to enjoy, as well as the Queen Elizabeth Temperate House.

The Savill Garden Visitor Centre.

❀ SCOTNEY CASTLE

Located near the delightful spa town of Tunbridge Wells in Kent, this 30-acre (12-hectare) Grade I Listed Historic Garden has one of the most romantic settings of any garden in the South-east of England. The central feature of the garden is the partially ruined medieval 'moated' manor house of Scotney Old Castle, which is positioned on a small lake in a valley setting. High above the lake and with fine views across the surrounding countryside complete with its oast houses stands Scotney New Castle, or simply Scotney Castle – a house in the Elizabethan style built in 1836 for owner Edward Hussey to a design by Anthony Salvin. At the same time as Salvin was working on the house, Hussey commissioned artist and landscape gardener W. S. Gilpin to fashion grounds around both the old and the new properties in the Picturesque style following the traditions laid down by William Kent in the eighteenth century. Gilpin's design had the old castle as its main focal point and he even persuaded Hussey to selectively demolish parts of the walls to accentuate its ruined nature. ▸

Woodland gardens provide all-year-round colour.

◀ Sloping upwards and away from the lake, fine woodland gardens were laid out to provide all-year-round colour and interest. Plants used included rhododendrons, magnolias and azaleas for spring, kalmias, wisteria and roses for summer and hydrangeas to carry both flowering and leaf colouring right through into autumn where they combined with Japanese maples, Persian ironwoods and North American liquidambars. Gilpin did more work on the terracing behind the new house, but Hussey took it on himself to furnish the rest of the valley using strong-form trees placed in dramatic positions.

Edward Hussey's grandson Christopher added much to the garden in the 1950s and 1960s and on his death in 1970 the estate was left to the National Trust, but it wasn't until after 2006, when his wife Betty passed away, that the house opened regularly to the public.

Although much of the woodland garden survives to this day, many of the original oaks, beeches, limes, yews, pines and cedars succumbed during the 1987 storm. Nearly thirty years on however, their replacements are beginning to mature and will soon punctuate the skyline just like their predecessors.

The garden today includes smaller features including herbaceous borders backed by roses and clematis and a herb garden in the castle forecourt. The 1-acre (0.4-hectare) walled kitchen garden is now back in production and early in the year snowdrops, primroses and daffodils are in profusion.

Medieval 'moated' manor house.

A magnificent white Wisteria in the courtyard.

❉ THE SECRET GARDENS OF SANDWICH

This delightful 3.5-acre (1.4-hectare) Edwin Lutyens and Gertrude Jekyll-designed garden surrounds The Salutation, a Lutyens manor house built in 1912 (now a hotel) and is hidden away behind the ancient town walls of Sandwich in Kent, hence the name. Neglected for twenty-five years, an extensive restoration and replanting programme for the garden was put in place after 2003 when owners Dom and Steph Parker took up residence. By 2007 they and their team of gardeners had done much to return the gardens to their former early twentieth-century glory and

Monty Don officially reopened them to the public in the same year.

Sadly, during the winter storms of 2013, the garden was flooded with over five million litres of sea water, which not only destroyed much of the planting but left its mark in terms of soil degradation too. However in the past two years Head Gardener Steve Edney and his team of gardeners have done wonders to get the garden back on track and it really is well worth visiting.

Many of Lutyens' traditional features are still in place, reworked and reinvigorated in places and these sit comfortably, ▸

Gertrude Jekyll-designed borders.

◀ even harmoniously, alongside more contemporary designs introduced by the Parkers and Edney since their arrival. Lutyens' original structure was built around a series of symmetrical garden rooms, each with a different theme and these still remain, for example in the White Garden where alliums and camassias stand out like stars against the surrounding dark evergreen hedges. Likewise in the Yellow Garden where yellow-flowering potentillas are augmented by the foliage of golden and variegated hollies, *Euonymus fortunei* cultivars and *Choisya ternata* 'Sundance'. The connection which holds both the old and the new styles together is the planting, slightly cottage garden and informal, but with borders full to overflowing with interesting and unusual plants alongside tried and tested colourful stalwarts.

This truly is a plant-lovers' garden and has been intelligently planted to ensure each month has something different to offer. The tropical gardens are replanted and altered each year, as many of the plants used are annuals, or so tender they would not survive an English winter, even on the South coast. Add to the mix a kitchen garden, vegetable garden, perennial borders heightened by obelisks of climbing roses, a laburnum walk and a small lake with an island and you can begin to see that although this garden may not be large, there is plenty to interest and inspire.

Garden rooms designed around colour.

The White Garden with alliums and camassias.

❀ SHEFFIELD PARK

Sheffield Park is located in the Sussex Weald at an elevation which ranges between 262 to 328 feet (80 to 100 metres) above sea-level. It is a Grade I Listed landscape extending in total to 120 acres (49 hectares). The garden, which is in essence a twentieth-century creation, overlays in part an eighteenth-century landscape, portions of which (including at least two of the four lakes which form the centrepiece to the garden) were designed by Lancelot 'Capability Brown' in around 1775 for John Baker Holroyd, later Earl of Sheffield. The family further extended and developed the landscape in the nineteenth century, but it was Lincolnshire brewer Arthur Gilstrap Soames who, having purchased the property in 1909, created much of what is on view today. Since 1953 the garden and park have been managed by the National Trust. Following the Great Storm of October 1987, which devastated the garden and its surrounding shelterbelts of trees, the Trust have taken a sensitive approach to restoration and have built on Soames' original plant collections, rather than move away from them.

It is around the four lakes, which are laid out in an inverted 'T' formation running away from the house (not National Trust), that the majority of the ornamental plantings occur. When Soames arrived the lakes were already bordered by billowing clumps of rhododendrons growing in the shade of exotic conifers planted by the 3rd Earl of Sheffield towards the end of the nineteenth century. It was seen then as a spring garden and in many ways it still is today, with glorious drifts ▶

Autumn colours around the lakes.

Billowing clouds of azaleas.

◀ of Lent lilies *Narcissus pseudonarcissus,* other old-fashioned daffodil hybrids and bluebells skirting around mass plantings of camellias, rhododendrons and 'Hinomayo' azaleas, however what Soames did was to turn Sheffield Park into a garden with strength and aesthetic appeal throughout the year.

Perhaps his greatest success was in the way he used woody plants already known for their vibrant autumn leaf colours such as Japanese maples, North American oaks, swamp cypresses, amelanchiers and nyssas to skilfully weave fiery tapestries which were mirrored in the nearby waters of the lakes.

Such was his success, that it is no exaggeration to say that even now a century on, the view in October from the cascade and bridge which separates the First and Middle Lakes is one of the finest garden vistas in Britain and encompasses a 360-degree kaleidoscope of reds, gold, orange and yellow all set to an evergreen foil of mature conifers and rhododendrons.

Middle Lake looking back to the house.

❧ SISSINGHURST

S issinghurst is possibly the best known and indeed best loved garden in England. On arrival, it is the fairytale sixteenth-century twin-turreted red-brick castle tower which greets you, just as it was for the garden's restorer Vita Sackville-West in April 1930. '... it was ... love at first sight. I saw what might be made of it ... Sleeping Beauty's castle ... a garden crying out for rescue'.

By 1932 the site was cleared and some of the gardens we recognise today were already laid out. Much of the design for the garden was drawn up by Vita Sackville-West's husband, Harold Nicolson. A 'straight ruler man', the structure was formal with long, straight paths running to all main points of the compass and each finishing with a 'full stop'– a seat, a statue, or possibly a specimen tree. However it was off these main axis routes, bordered by walls or tight-clipped hedges of yew or beech, that the garden was allowed to unfold with gateways, arches and ▸

The White Garden.

◀ openings leading into a series of themed 'garden rooms', in much the same way that school classrooms used to lead off a main corridor.

If this all sounds rather utilitarian, be assured Sissinghurst is anything but. The whole point is the reveal, the surprise, indeed the delight at the way just a few steps off the main routes brings you to a range of beautiful and very different interiors: The Rose Garden burgeoning with fragrant old-fashioned varieties beloved by Vita,

the south-facing purple, violet-blue and magenta borders, the orange, red and yellow Cottage Garden, the Herb Garden with its camomile seat and the sublime simplicity of the White Garden, perhaps the most famous English garden of all. Created in 1950, it has since been copied the world over and yet it is to the original that we return for inspiration, white-flowering *Lilium regale,* irises, delphiniums and rambling roses all foiled by grey and glaucous foliaged hostas, artemisia and *Pyrus salicifolia* 'Pendula'. ▶

The garden from the tower.

Sixteenth-century red-brick castle tower.

❉ SISSINGHURST

◀ Yes of course, Sissinghurst was not the first 'garden of rooms'; Johnston's Hidcote in Gloucestershire preceded it by a good few years and the Mawson and Cory gardens at Dyffryn are even earlier, but somehow neither have the emotional romanticism that Vita Sackville-West and Harold Nicolson managed to achieve at Sissinghurst. Here is a blue-skied, verdant green England, as viewed perhaps through the misty-eyed reminiscences of someone who 'stayed on' after the pink drained from the map of the world and now yearns to be home again.

The series of 'garden rooms'.

✿ STANDEN

Standen House, designed by Arts & Crafts architect Philip Webb, is perhaps the main reason for most visits to this National Trust property, and the interior, with its William Morris adornments, is an absolute delight. Nevertheless the garden, with its sweeping views south across the Medway Valley to the Ashdown Forest, is undoubtedly worthy of visitation in its own right.

The house was built in the early 1890s for prosperous London solicitor James Beale, his wife Margaret and their seven children, and for the next seventy years remained the Beale family home. Although it sits on the side of the hill, it does not dominate the landscape and is completely unpretentious. Built out of local sandstone quarried on site, and with the care and attention to detail that only the Arts & Crafts movement could achieve, even earlier buildings such as nearby fifteenth-century Hollybush Farm were not neglected, or worse destroyed, but gathered into the Beale fold and carefully preserved around a 'village green'.

The Beales started planting the 12-acre (4.8-hectare) garden in the spring of 1891, with ornamental trees, a regular structure of yew hedging and the beginnings of a kitchen garden. They consulted London landscape architect G. B. Simpson who (with some intervention by architect Philip Webb) came up with a geometrical layout ▸

Amelanchier lamarckii on the croquet lawn.

Avenue of fine camellias.

◀ of compartments, but then the whole was softened at the edges with informal plantings and a gentle transition from garden to surrounding landscape. Perhaps one of the most enchanting features at Standen is the Quarry garden, where yellow-flowering *Rhododendron luteum* fills the air with fragrance, climbing hydrangea *Hydrangea anomala subsp. petiolaris* softens the rock face and verdant ferns jostle for poolside position in the warm moist atmosphere.

Espalier fruit trees remain from the original kitchen garden, which has been lovingly restored by the Trust in recent years. Just along from the conservatory and growing on the walls of the house is an original Banksian rose *Rosa banksiae* 'Lutea' coupled with wisteria and clematis. Terrace borders below the house are full of interesting herbaceous plantings mixed with flowering shrubs and *Rosa* 'Sanders White Rambler' and are an absolute delight in summer. For spring there is a rhododendron dell, an avenue of fine camellias, specimen *Amelanchier lamarckii* trees on the edge of the croquet lawn and lawns full of narcissus, followed by snakeshead fritillaries and orchids. Autumn too is well represented with an excellent collection of Japanese maples providing strikingly vibrant leaf colours.

Bluebells in the surrounding woodland.

✿ ST MARY'S HOUSE AND GARDENS

Set in the heart of the South Downs National Park in West Sussex, St Mary's House is a beautiful fifteenth-century Grade I Listed timber-framed medieval house, which was once used as a pilgrim inn. The house, with its fine panelled interior, is open to the public, but surrounding the house are over 5 acres (2 hectares) of delightful gardens which have been sensitively designed to be in keeping with this historic setting.

The approach to the house is along a short avenue of lime trees which leads into a small gravel garden uniformly laid out with tight clipped, low box hedging, offset by colourful bedding. From here, a pretty stone bridge with balustrading crosses a stream and then enters into the Topiary Garden where characterful animals and birds have been clipped out of yew and box. Beyond the bridge and directly in front of the house, the garden opens out into a series of beds and borders, which in summer are full to overflowing with flamboyantly-coloured hollyhocks, in some cases over 6ft (1.8m) tall. ▸

St Mary's House.

◀ A yew tunnel leads through a stone arch and to the atmospheric ivy-clad Monk's Walk and then onto the upper lawn which is enclosed by herbaceous borders, while the lower lawn has clipped yew hedges, roses and a fine specimen of the 'living fossil' or maidenhair tree, *Ginkgo biloba*. Beyond this lies a bog garden and stream.

The former productive 'Lost Gardens of Bramber' have recently been imaginatively restored and this Victorian 'Secret Garden' now includes a reclaimed 140-ft- (40-m) long fruit wall, as well as heated pineapple pits and a fully-functioning stove house. The original Boulton and Paul potting shed has been turned into a rural museum which includes many horticultural implements collected from the surrounding family farms. Nearby, a rose garden commemorates both Her Majesty the Queen's Golden and Diamond Jubilees and a perennial border is planted in memory of the late Queen Mother. In the Terracotta Garden there are box parterres and a central fountain which is surrounded by colourful herbaceous borders.

The unusual circular English Poetry Garden (formerly an orchard) has been re-landscaped and includes a semicircular pergola, an inner circle of yew, a bust of Lord Byron and a circular boardwalk upon which poems are displayed. There is also a new landscaped water garden with an island and waterfall. Beyond this lies a woodland walk with a huge willow and swathes of bluebells, primulas and other native wild flowers.

Central fountain in the Terracotta Garden.

The Walled Garden.

❈ SUSSEX PRAIRIES GARDEN

Covering 8 acres (3.2 hectares), this delightful prairie-style garden set in the heart of the Sussex Weald, contains over 30,000 plants of over 800 different varieties and is a kaleidoscope of colour, form and texture from June right through until October. As such it is not only a delight for visitors, but is also a haven for butterflies, birds and insects.

Enveloped by mature oak trees, the garden at Sussex Prairies is comprised of beds and borders which are laid out in a series of interlocking arcs, rather like the shape of a spiralling nautilus shell and deliberately designed to mirror the curvaceous lines of the nearby South Downs. They were first laid out in May 2008 and collectively have now developed into a truly extraordinary garden, with each border containing huge, sumptuous ever-changing drifts of herbaceous perennials and grasses in thoughtful combinations that are designed to inspire and excite. As the majority of colours are deliberately soft and muted to complement the surrounding natural landscape, when bright drifts of gold or orange do occur their vibrancy appears doubly effective, especially when contrasting against the hornbeam hedges that bisect some of the arcs. ▶

Sumptuous drifts of herbaceous perennials and grasses.

❀ SUSSEX PRAIRIES GARDEN

◀ The borders serve as a living catalogue of plants used by owners Paul and Pauline McBride, both for their garden design business and as propagation stock for their excellent nursery which is located on site. Paul and Pauline have been creating gardens for over thirty years, both in the wilds of Rajasthan and in Luxembourg.

Paul trained in horticulture in Scotland and Pauline has a natural artistic flair, so the perfect combination for designing gardens! It was while living in Luxembourg that they both became inspired by the work of Dutch landscape designer Piet Oudolf and his influence can be seen throughout their latest garden creation here in Sussex. ▶

Artistic flair for plant combinations.

✿ SUSSEX PRAIRIES GARDEN

◀ Some of the borders are created entirely using grasses and the colours which they bring to the garden pallet are truly astonishing, ranging from pink *Miscanthus sinensis* 'Flamingo' to bronze and white-flowered *Stipa gigantea*, both of which are at their best when low sun illuminates their plumes at either ends of the day. Complementing the grasses are bold perennial swathes which include pink-flowering *Persicaria* sp., golden-yellow Rudbeckias and purple-orange Echinacea. As a finishing touch to a garden that approaches perfection, look out for the regular art installations, which can vary from metal silhouettes of bison (ranging the prairies) to giant heads appearing among the plants!

Grasses such as stipa and miscanthus abound.

✿ TITSEY PLACE

Titsey is one of the largest surviving historic estates in Surrey. The house dates back to the mid-sixteenth century and is built on the site of an even earlier property, although the first impression today is of a comfortable early nineteenth century house, set within parkland laid out in the picturesque style.

Given its beautiful location, nestled into the wooded escarpment of the North Downs, which rise to some 800 feet (243 metres) above sea-level, it is hard to believe that Titsey lies no more than 20 miles from the centre of London and it is only the proximity of the M25 motorway that suggests anything has changed here for centuries. For the majority of the past 400 hundred years the property has been the home of the Gresham and Leverson Gower family and today it is the trustees of the Titsey Foundation, a charitable trust, which manages the estate and opens the house, gardens and surrounding park and woodland to visitors.

The Historic Grade II-Listed Garden extends to some 18 acres (7.2 hectares) and ▸

Fine views from the upper terrace.

Titsey Place.

Sweeping lawns run down to lakes.

◀ is both charming and varied in its design. Perhaps one of its finest features is the 1-acre (0.4-hectare) Victorian walled kitchen garden which was completely restored in 1996 to provide an authentic illustration of Victorian horticultural techniques. Espaliered fruit on the walls includes pears, plums and apples, in front of which are deep borders filled with old-fashioned roses and annuals. Box-edged paths provide classic segmentation to the garden and two metal gazebos provide both height and structure. Within the productive beds unusual varieties of vegetables, salad crops, strawberries and herbs are joined by around 100 different varieties of tomatoes raised from seed collected from around the world. There is a cutting garden, which is at its best in summer and greenhouses used to grow fine collections of alstroemerias, pelargoniums and peaches. A centrally positioned glass conservatory houses a wide range of exotic plants and orchids, some of which date back to shortly after the Second World War. Beyond the walls the garden is a mixture of rose gardens, a modern Etruscan temple and formal lawns, dotted with magnificent mature specimen trees, which run down to two lakes (one with an island) divided by a bridge and cascade and fringed by water-loving bog plants.

From the upper terrace there are fine views of the surrounding woodland, with its 4 miles (6.4 kilometres) of public footpaths, and across the Surrey countryside to the Darent Valley and the South Downs beyond.

Lakes are divided by a bridge and cascade.

THE VALLEY GARDENS WINDSOR

Considered by some to be one of the best examples of the 'natural' gardening style in England, the Valley Gardens in Windsor Great Park are comprised of a series of majestic woodland gardens set beneath canopies of beautiful mature trees (some centuries old) and with delightful views to Virginia Water Lake. The area has few introduced architectural embellishments or artefacts and the only other feature besides the plants is the topography itself – large tracts of undulating sandy soil divided by a number of sweeping valleys, sometimes steep-sided, sometimes shallow.

The garden was conceived and created after the Second World War by royal gardener and Deputy Ranger of Windsor Great Park Sir Eric Savill and his head gardener Hope Findlay, with the blessing of King George VI and Queen Elizabeth. Rather ingeniously it has been suggested that the Valley Gardens were initially nothing more than an overflow area for plants once lack of space became a problem in nearby Savill Garden. In fact, this was no mere 'dumping ground' for surplus plants; a great deal of thought went into the garden's development. Inspired by the area's unique parallel valleys and the large scale of the landscape, Savill and Findlay deliberately chose to plant large numbers of specific plant genera all together in one place. ▶

The Punch Bowl.

Spring azaleas abound.

◀ Perhaps the best example of this is within the valley known as the Punch Bowl. Here the sides of a natural amphitheatre have been clothed in hundreds of evergreen Japanese Kurume azaleas. From mid-April until June they flower prolifically beneath a canopy of Japanese maples and the effect when viewed from the bottom of the bowl is quite simply sublime. Large-scale plantings in other parts of the garden include deciduous azaleas and there is an excellent collection of Japanese flowering cherries too.

In all the Valley Gardens cover 220 acres (89 hectares) and can genuinely be described by that sometimes overworked phrase 'a garden for all seasons'. Accompanying the azaleas and cherries in spring are camellias, rhododendrons, magnolias and many other flowering trees and shrubs, with great swathes of daffodils blooming alongside.

Massed plantings of hydrangeas are the highlight of summer and they in turn herald the arrival of magnificent autumn leaf colours from oaks, maples, birches, sweet gums and tupelos, which collectively light up the woodland.

Even in the depths of winter there is plenty to see with witch hazels and drifts of heather in flower among the dwarf conifers in the Heather Garden.

A garden for all seasons.

❋ WAKEHURST PLACE

Across the lake to Wakehurst Place.

Wakehurst Place is situated among some of the finest scenery of the High Sussex Weald. The estate has a long history dating back to the time of the Normans and at the centre of the garden is a fine Elizabethan mansion; however its botanical history is relatively recent.

Wakehurst was purchased by Gerald Loder (later Lord Wakehurst) in 1902. Loder was an enthusiastic and knowledgeable plantsman who subscribed to several overseas plant-collecting expeditions in the early years of the twentieth century. In all he spent thirty-three years developing the gardens at Wakehurst and built up a fine plant collection in the process. After his death in 1936 the estate was purchased by Sir Henry Price, who continued the gardens' development until his death in 1963 when the garden was bequeathed to the National Trust, who in 1965 leased it to the Royal Botanic Garden at Kew on a ninety-nine-year lease. Since then Kew has transformed the garden into a modern, internationally admired botanic garden which is now at the forefront of plant conservation across the world.

The Great Storm of October 1987 caused much damage, but it did bring the opportunity to rationalise the collections and to begin again in some areas. Today, well-managed collections of hardy plants can be found throughout Wakehurst's 180 acres (73 hectares). Plants are grouped together, either by related genera or by geographical origin, so that visitors and those studying the collection can gain an understanding of regional plant associations, plant diversity and how plants interact with each other in their natural habitats.

While this may all sound somewhat scientific, it in no way negates the pleasing aesthetic of Wakehurst. The garden is a beautiful place to visit at any time of year. There is a rock garden full of alpines and dwarf plants, a heath garden, winter ▶

Across the lake.

Early spring at Wakehurst.

◀ garden, sheltered walled garden, Southern Hemisphere Garden, Bog Garden with fine collections of irises and candelabra primulas, Himalayan Glade with superb displays of rhododendrons, camellias and magnolias and a pinetum.

Opened in 2000, the Millennium Seed Bank (parts of which are accessible to the public) already conserves around 10 per cent of the world's flora in the form of viable seed, which could be propagated in the event of extinction in the wild.

Beyond the exotic plantings the estate also has extensive areas of woodland designated as a Site of Special Scientific Interest (SSSI) which provides valuable habitats for native flora, fungi and fauna.

Rhododendrons in the Bog Garden.

❋ WEALD & DOWNLAND
OPEN AIR MUSEUM

Founded in 1967, the Weald & Downland Open Air Museum is comprised of fifty original historic buildings, all of which have been rescued from destruction, restored and painstakingly rebuilt on the Museum's 40-acre (16-hectare) site. The buildings mostly originate from Sussex, Kent, Hampshire and Surrey and represent more than 600 years of history from the medieval era through to late Victorian.

Set in the heart of the South Downs National Park, part of the success of the Museum is the peace and tranquillity found in this beautiful unspoilt corner of Sussex. Indeed it is the rural nature of the landscape that so perfectly grounds and places this eclectic assortment of buildings, which in reality would never have stood 'cheek by jowl'. On a warm summer morning, with just the rhythmic sound of the working watermill grinding flour and the occasional blow of billhook cleaving chestnut, this is as near as any of us are ever likely to get to travelling back in time.

Receiving no regular governmental or local authority funding, the museum depends largely on volunteers and one of their tasks is to maintain the six period gardens, which between them show the transition of gardens and gardening from ▸

Over 600 years of history.

◀ the early sixteenth through to the late nineteenth century. The earliest gardens on display are almost entirely functional, producing food, medicines and plants for utilitarian purposes, such as dyeing and strewing. To our modern-day eye these early gardens are 'full of weeds', but plants such as chickweed, fat hen and nettles formed part of medieval daily diet, and groundsel and burdock were medicinally valuable.

The museum gardens demonstrate how, as the centuries passed, plants were increasingly grown for their aesthetic qualities. Each of the six gardens not only represent a moment in history, but also the social status of the householder at that time.

The gardens include a recreation of a Tudor yeoman farmer's garden from the 1540s growing vegetables and herbs detailed in *The Fromond List* – a cookery manuscript from that period. An early seventeenth-century garden shows that carrots were white (orange carrots came later). An 1810 Toll House garden has around 30 per cent of the plot given over to herbaceous flowering plants and a railway worker's cottage from the late Victorian period displays rotational cropping of vegetables in the back garden and in the front, a typical cottage garden containing a mixture of herbs such as sage, rosemary and thyme and flowers including iris, aster, forget-me-not and Sweet William.

Modern-day weeds were once useful plants.

Stepping back in time.

❋ WEST DEAN GARDENS

There have been gardens at West Dean since 1622 when the original manor house was built. The current house dates from 1804 and it was then that the gardens were enlarged, parkland laid out and the kitchen garden moved to its present location and enclosed by walls. William James purchased the property in 1891 and commissioned architect and garden designer Harold Peto, who among other things designed the magnificent 300-ft- (100-metre-) long pergola on the North Lawn. On his father's death in 1912, Edward James inherited the estate and although he enjoyed the gardens he spent much time overseas, the gardens gradually entering a period of decline.

It was the Great Storm of October 1987 which became the catalyst for the revival of this remarkable Grade II Listed Historic Garden. Since then an imaginative restoration has been undertaken and the 90 acres (36 hectares) of grounds are now subdivided into four distinct areas: the gardens entrance, the walled kitchen garden, the pleasure grounds and St Roche's Arboretum (which accounts for some 49 acres (20 hectares) of the whole).

Despite being the smallest area by acreage, it is probably the walled gardens which are the highlight of any visit to West Dean today. To quote Anna Pavord's words from the Independent, 'If you want to see fruit and vegetables growing in profusion, ▶

Succulents on display.

The Kitchen Garden orchard.

◀ this is the garden to visit; I have never been in a kitchen garden so rich, so profuse, so well ordered, so tempting!'

The thirteen restored Victorian glasshouses are immaculate and home to a huge variety of edible plants including peaches, peppers, chillies, cucumbers, melons and aubergines, plus ornamental collections of succulents, cacti, sub-tropical plants, orchids and ferns. Surrounding the kitchen garden is over 1 mile of walls, some crinkle-crankled and mostly covered in trained apples, pears, cherries and plums, all excellently labelled. As well as wall-trained there are free-standing orchards and fruit trees trained around interestingly shaped metal frames. Elsewhere within the walls there are magnificent vegetable and soft fruit beds and a glorious cutting garden producing stunning displays of flowers from late spring until autumn.

Beyond the walls lies the ornamental grounds, designed around West Dean House, now an Arts & Crafts college. Peto's pergola is one of the largest in Britain and smothered in lush plantings of wisteria, clematis, honeysuckle and climbing roses. The spring garden boasts a laburnum tunnel and ornamental flint-work bridges spanning the River Lavant. Beyond lies rolling parkland and St Roche's Arboretum, carpeted in spring with wild daffodils.

Harold Peto's pergola.

❈ WINKWORTH ARBORETUM

Winkworth is without doubt one of South East England's finest tree and shrub collections. Situated south of the delightful old market town of Godalming, and just a stone's throw from what was Gertrude Jekyll's home and garden at Munstead Wood (privately owned), it is probably most famous for its stunning autumnal leaf colours, delivered in the main by thoughtful plant combinations of maples, rowans, tupelo trees and dogwoods. However Winkworth is much more than a garden for only one season and deserves to be far better known than it currently is.

The arboretum is the creation of Dr Wilfred Fox who purchased the steeply sloping 110-acre (44-hectare) valley site in 1937 from actress Beatrice Lilley. It had until that point been rather neglected. The topography making it unsuitable for agricultural cultivation, it had been left as woodland – predominantly oak with a few areas of sweet chestnut coppice. In the valley bottom was a fishing lake with an attractive timber boathouse, beyond which the land evened out into a series of gentle rolling hills. To Dr Fox this was the perfect site to assemble a large-scale collection of ornamental and exotic trees and shrubs all set within a semi-natural setting. Although originally an amateur gardener and botanist, he had a passion for woody plants and was inspired by collections already established at Sheffield Park, Exbury, Westonbirt, Kew and Hilliers. Over the years he became an acknowledged expert in this field, specialising in the genus *Sorbus* which includes rowan and whitebeam. From 1937 until his death in 1962 he amassed a remarkable collection of trees and shrubs from around the world, helped from 1952 by the National Trust to whom he bequeathed ▶

Across the lake to the escarpment.

Nyssa sylvatica in full autumn glory.

◀ two thirds of the land, whereupon the Trust acquired the final third in 1957.

Today Dr Fox's collection, carefully managed and expanded by the National Trust, is a 'tour de force' and one which not only works scientifically but aesthetically too. A National Collection (NCCPG – Plant Heritage) of *Sorbus* is at its heart, but fine collections of holly, birch and magnolia all add to the mix, while Winkworth-raised cultivars such as *Acer davidii* 'Madeline Spitta', named after Dr Fox's friend and colleague from his time on the 'Roads Beautifying Committee', reaffirm Winkworth's botanical credentials.

In spring bright splashes of colour from mass plantings of camellia, rhododendron and azalea, overhung by flowering cherries, spill down the slopes towards the lake. If you are lucky enough to be there on a late April morning, when the sun's warmth fills the valley with hyacinth-like fragrance from sublime drifts of bluebells, it is hard to imagine a more perfect place in England.

A glade of Japanese maples.